THE
JOURNEY
TO A
NEW LIFE

A BOOK OF THE
NEW MESSAGE
FROM GOD

THE
JOURNEY
TO A
NEW LIFE

AS REVEALED TO

Marshall Vian Summers

THE
JOURNEY
TO A
NEW LIFE

Edited by Darlene Mitchell
Cover and interior: Designed by Reed Summers

ISBN: 978-1-942293-42-2 (POD)
ISBN: 978-1-942293-43-9 (ebook)
NKL POD Version 7.06
Library of Congress Control Number: 2018968001

Publisher's Cataloging-in-Publication
(Prepared by The Donohue Group, Inc.)

Names: Summers, Marshall Vian, author.
Title: The journey to a new life / as revealed to Marshall Vian Summers.
Description: Boulder, CO : New Knowledge Library, the publishing imprint
    of The Society for the New Message, [2019] | "A book of the New Message
from God."
Identifiers: ISBN 9781942293422 (POD) | ISBN 9781942293439 (ebook)
Subjects: LCSH: Society for the New Message--Doctrines. | Spiritual life.
    | Self-actualization (Psychology)--Religious aspects. | Mystical union.
    | Knowledge, Theory of (Religion)
Classification: LCC BP605.S58 S86 2019 (print) | LCC BP605.S58 (ebook)
    | DDC 299/.93--dc23

The Journey to a New Life is a book of the New Message from God and is published by New Knowledge Library, the publishing imprint of The Society for the New Message. The Society is a religious non-profit organization dedicated to presenting and teaching a New Message for humanity. The books of New Knowledge Library can be ordered at www.newknowledgelibrary.org, your local bookstore and at many other online retailers.

The New Message is being studied in more than 30 languages in over 90 countries. *The Journey to a New Life* is being translated into the many languages of our world by a dedicated group of volunteer student translators from around the world. These translations will all be available online at www.newmessage.org.

The Society for the New Message
P.O. Box 1724   Boulder, CO 80306-1724
(303) 938-8401   (800) 938-3891
011 303 938 84 01 (International)   (303) 938-1214 (fax)
newmessage.org   newknowledgelibrary.org
email: society@newmessage.org

We shall speak of God, the Higher Authority.

The Higher Authority is speaking to you now, speaking through the Angelic Presence, speaking to a part of you that is the very center and source of your Being.

The Higher Authority has a Message for the world, and for each person in the world.

The Higher Authority is calling to you, calling to you down through the Ancient Corridors of your mind, calling to you beyond your beliefs and your preoccupations.

For God has spoken again and the Word and the Sound are in the world.

From *God Has Spoken Again,*
Chapter 3: The Engagement

THE
JOURNEY
TO A
NEW LIFE

TABLE OF CONTENTS

INTRODUCTION

$\mathcal{T}$*he Journey to a New Life* is a book of Revelation given by the Creator of all life to the human family through the Messenger Marshall Vian Summers.

Throughout history, God has given Revelation and Wisdom to meet the growing needs of our world at great turning points in the evolution of humanity. Now God is speaking again, delivering a New Revelation to meet the critical needs of humanity as it faces Great Waves of environmental, political and economic change and contact with a Greater Community of intelligent life in the universe.

God's progressive Revelation is continuing anew through a New Message from God, of which *The Journey to a New Life* is but a part. The words of this text are a direct communication from the Creator of all life, translated into human language by the Angelic Presence that watches over this world, and then spoken through the Messenger Marshall Vian Summers, who has given over 30 years of his life to this process of Revelation.

The New Message from God is an original communication from God to the heart of every person on Earth. It is not for one nation, one tribe or one religion alone. It is a Message for the entire world, a world facing very different needs and challenges from those of ancient times.

This communication is here to ignite the spiritual power of humanity, to sound God's calling for unity amongst the world's nations and religions, and to prepare humanity for a radically changing world and for its destiny in a larger universe of intelligent life.

The New Message from God speaks on nearly every aspect of life facing people today. It is the largest Revelation ever given to humanity, given now to a literate world of global communication and growing global awareness. Never before has there been a Divine

Revelation of this size, given by God to all people of the world at once, in the lifetime of the Messenger.

Yet the New Message from God has not entered the world through the existing religious authorities and institutions of today. It has not come to the leaders of religion or to those who garner fame and recognition. Instead, it has been given to a humble man chosen and sent into the world for this one task, to be a Messenger for this New Message for humanity.

The Messenger has walked a long and difficult road to bring the New Message from God to you and to the world. The process of Revelation began in 1982 and continues to this day. The Messenger's story is one of perseverance, humility and lifelong service to others. His presence in the world today represents an opportunity to know him and receive the Revelation directly from him.

At the center of the New Message is the original Voice of Revelation, which has spoken the words of every book of the New Message. Never before has the Voice of Revelation, the Voice that spoke to the Messengers and prophets of the past, been recorded in its original purity and made available to each person to hear and to experience for themselves. In this way, the Word and the Sound of God's Revelation are in the world.

In this remarkable process of spoken Revelation, the Presence of God communicates beyond words to the Angelic Assembly that oversees the world. The Assembly then translates this communication into human language and speaks all as one through their Messenger, whose voice becomes the vehicle for this greater Voice—the Voice of Revelation.

The words of this Voice have been recorded in audio form, transcribed and are now available in the books of the New Message. In addition, the original audio recordings of the Voice of Revelation are available for all to hear. In this way, the purity of God's original spoken Message is preserved and given to all people in the world.

INTRODUCTION

At this time, The Messenger is engaged in compiling over three decades of spoken Revelation into a final and complete text—The One Book of the New Message from God. This book of Revelation will ultimately be divided into six volumes and possibly more. Each volume will contain two or more books, and each book will be organized by chapter and verse. Therefore, the New Message from God will be structured in the following way: Volume > Book > Chapter > Verse.

The Journey to a New Life is the sixth book of Volume 1 of the New Message from God and *The Journey to a New Life* contains 14 individual revelations (chapters) revealed to the Messenger at different times. The Messenger has compiled these revelations into the text you see today.

In order to bring this spoken communication into written form, slight textual and grammatical adjustments were made by the Messenger. This was requested of him by the Angelic Assembly to aid the understanding of the reader and to convey the Message according to the grammatical standards of the written English language.

In some instances, the Messenger has inserted a word not originally spoken in the Revelation. When present, you will often find this inserted word in brackets. Consider these bracketed words as direct clarifications by the Messenger, placed in the text by him alone in order to ensure that ambiguities in the spoken communication do not cause confusion or incorrect interpretations of the text.

In some cases, the Messenger has removed a word to aid the readability of the text. This was usually done in the case of certain conjunctions (words such as *and, but*) that made the text unnecessarily awkward or grammatically incorrect.

The Messenger alone has made these slight changes and only to convey the original spoken communication with the greatest clarity possible. None of the original meaning or intention of the communication has been altered.

The text of this book has been structured by the Messenger into verse. Each verse roughly signals the beginning or ending of a distinct message point communicated by the Source.

The verse structure of the text allows the reader to access the richness of the content and those subtle messages that may otherwise be missed in longer paragraphs of text that convey multiple topics. In this way, each topic and idea communicated by the Source is given its own standing, allowing it to speak from the page directly to the reader. The Messenger has determined that structuring the text in verse is the most efficacious and faithful way of rendering the original spoken revelations of the New Message.

Through this text, we are witnessing the process of preparation and compilation being undertaken by the Messenger, in his own time, by his own hands. This stands in stark contrast to the fact that the former great traditions were rarely put into written form by their Messengers, leaving the original messages vulnerable to alteration and corruption over time.

Here the Messenger seals in purity the texts of God's New Message and gives them to you, to the world and to all people in the future. Whether this book is opened today or 500 years from now, God's original communication will speak from these pages with the same intimacy, purity and power as it did the day it was first spoken.

Though it appears to be a book in the hand, *The Journey to a New Life* is something far greater. It is a calling and a communication from the Heart of God to you. In the pages of this book, God's Presence calls to you and to all people, calling for you to awaken from the dream and nightmare of living in Separation apart from your Source, calling to the presence of "Knowledge," the deeper spiritual Intelligence that lives within you, waiting to be discovered.

INTRODUCTION

The Journey to a New Life is part of a living communication from God to humanity. Remarkably, you have found the New Message from God, or it has found you. It is no coincidence that this is the case. This opens the next chapter in the mystery of your life and of your presence in the world at this time. The door opens before you. You need only enter to begin.

As you enter more deeply into the Revelation, the impact on your life will grow, bringing a greater experience of clarity, inner certainty and true direction to your life. In time, your questions will be answered as you find growing freedom from self-doubt, inner conflict and the restraints of the past. Here the Creator of all life is speaking to you directly, revealing to you the greater life that you were always destined to live.

The Society for the New Message from God

CHAPTER 1
_____

THE AWAKENING

As revealed to
Marshall Vian Summers
on October 20, 2008
in Boulder, Colorado

Regardless of your circumstances or nationality or cultural heritage, there are certain questions that are fundamental to your existence here. And once certain requirements of life have been met—the basic requirements of food, clothing, shelter and security; and some psychological requirements of relationship, companionship and employment—then you come upon a greater set of needs.

Some people will only come upon these greater needs later in life, after they have tasted the pleasures and the sorrows of the world sufficiently that they realize there is no fulfillment there for them. While work and relationships and family are important, there is something more important that begins to emerge in their lives.

For certain people, these questions arise much earlier in the formation of their personality and their establishment in the world at the outset. They are preoccupied with a deeper set of needs. They need to have a real sense of why they are in the world, what they are here to do, who they are here to meet and what they must cultivate and develop within themselves to experience and to express a greater purpose in life.

Clearly, in the world there is a struggle for survival. There is a struggle for social acceptance. There is a struggle to make a living and have a sustainable job or career. There is a struggle to establish oneself and to maintain stability within the changing circumstances of life. All of these are very fundamental and represent a set of needs, but there is a deeper set of needs, needs that not only fulfill the basic requirements of life, but really establish a greater sense of purpose, meaning and destiny in life.

These questions are not questions that the intellect alone can resolve. You may have theories or ideas, or be entertaining the ideas of great thinkers or philosophers or other influential people that you might be aware of, but really these questions must be taken to a greater authority within you.

The intellect that you think with every day, that determines your experience to such a great extent, this is a product of your being in the world. It has been developed over time into a sophisticated mechanism for communication and evaluation.

But your deeper purpose was created before you came into the world. Your destiny was established before you came into the world. It is not the providence of the intellect.

Your intellect will have to concern itself with how you are going to set your life in a higher direction and all the particulars that will have to be considered and dealt with along the way. But the meaning, the purpose and direction of this greater purpose are established at a deeper level.

This inquiry cannot be momentary. It cannot merely arise at times of great disappointment, confusion or disillusionment because it is a very great inquiry. It is not something you can entertain for a week or a month and hope to really gain momentum and progress here.

This requires a kind of shift within yourself as if an invisible switch has been thrown, and all of a sudden another door has opened in your inner experience and you are entertaining things that before perhaps you only thought of intermittently or very infrequently, and now they become an abiding set of questions and concerns.

There is a deeper Knowledge within you, a deeper Intelligence that is not the product of your being in the world, that is not a construction of social influences and patterns of thought and behavior. It is Intelligence that is in the world, but not of the world. We call this Knowledge because it is related to your experience of profound insight and awareness.

Your need for this Knowledge will grow once you begin to entertain a deeper set of questions about your life. You will realize that the intellect has only ideas, and even if they seem to be very well considered ideas, or ideas with a long tradition with many commentators, they are still only ideas.

But you are living with something like a living Presence within yourself that is not really the product of ideas. You will have ideas about it. You will try to understand it. You will try to look for evidence or commentary regarding it from other important people, and that is appropriate. But you are still dealing with something beyond the realm of the intellect—a deeper manifestation, a deeper sense of purpose, a deeper and greater set of forces.

Here you must accept the mystery of your life and accept that you will feel a little out of control regarding it. You will feel a little insecure regarding it because it is something greater that you can only follow and learn from. Do not tax your mind trying to encompass this reality, for you will not be able to do so. As it grows in scope and experience for you, you will see that it will constantly transcend and overwhelm your ideas and assumptions.

You must approach this not as a consumer, not as someone who is trying to get what they want, but instead approach this in a sacred manner, for now you are dealing with a sacred power. This requires an emphasis on giving yourself as opposed to taking things for yourself.

The needs of the soul must be met by a greater set of powers. Who you are, and why you are here at this time, and why you are designed the way you are, with all of the uniqueness of your mind and characteristics, is connected to a greater purpose, and this purpose is not your invention.

Here you are not creating your reality. You are allowing your reality to emerge within you. And you are learning about it step by step, in stages, and shifting your life to accommodate this greater power so that it may move within you and express itself through you.

This is not a form of entertainment. This is not an intellectual pursuit. This is not a hobby or a fascination. This is the real current of your life, a deeper current that runs beneath the realm of the intellect, like a golden thread that passes through a complex fabric. It is like the copper wire that carries the current even though the wire itself is greatly concealed by all that encases it.

You will begin to feel a deeper need to know, not just to understand but to know something. Your life is passing you by. The clock is ticking. You are using up your time, your energy, your life force. It is being spent often recklessly, sometimes inappropriately. It is being spent rapidly. This time is precious. Your energy and life force are precious, and you are spending them rapidly. What are you doing? Are you just passing the time trying to stay stimulated and happy and comfortable, or is your time really being invested wisely and appropriately?

Are you living the life you know you were meant to live? If not, then this requires a deep evaluation, a self-examination, an objective review of your activities, your relationships, your involvements— where you live, who you are with; your activities, your goals, your hobbies, everything. Put everything out to be reconsidered. For they are all drawing energy from you. You are spending rapidly for them.

Are you where you need to be? Are you with the people you really need to be with? Is your work serving your development or supporting your development appropriately? Are your relationships moving in the direction that you really need to move? Do you share a higher purpose with the people you are now associated with? Are you taking care of your mental and physical health appropriately? Are you in the right place with the right people for the right purpose? These are all very useful questions to help you carry out this deep evaluation.

Here it is important not to look for consensus or agreement with other people, for if they are not feeling this deeper movement, they will not understand it. They will not agree to it. They will question you. They will cast doubt upon you. They will say, "What is the matter with you? You used to be such a fun person and now you are so serious." And they will want you to do the things that you did with them before, or things that they want you to do for their sake. They will not recognize and honor the deeper stirrings in your soul. Do not share your experiences with them. Do not share your inspiration with them, for in most cases they will discourage you.

You must seek now a different kind of relationship with people who are undergoing a very similar process of awakening within themselves, people who are beginning to stir from a long and troubled sleep. You need them now to bear witness to the process that is happening within yourself. Your life is being stirred by a deeper set of needs and by the emergence of a greater purpose.

It will change your values. It will change your priorities. Instead of constant stimulation and avoidance, you will want to experience yourself and where you are. You will seek quiet more than stimulation, honesty in relationships more than entertainment. You will want to know instead of seeking to escape from what you know.

It is as if you have turned 180 degrees and now everything feels different, and your relationship and position with everything is different. A deeper set of needs is emerging, and they require your attention and support. They require others who are capable of honoring this within you, without giving it definition or explanation.

It is as if you have turned a corner in life. Somehow you turned a corner and now you are moving in a slightly different direction. And even though you appear to be the same, and perhaps your circumstances have not changed very much, something inside has really changed, has reset your life and has altered your relationship with the universe in some small, but very significant way.

Many people talk about great change in their lives, but really when great change happens, it is imperceptible. And you know that a great change has occurred because you are feeling so very different about everything. Otherwise, change is a momentary experience. It generates a lot of conversation, a lot of excitement perhaps, but nothing really has changed.

The big change is imperceptible. It happens at a deeper level. It is not just a re-evaluation or a new experience. Something really has shifted on the inside at a level beyond the realm of the intellect, and now the intellect must catch up and re-adapt itself and re-adjust.

Much of what you will be going through within these early stages is a readjustment to a change that has already taken place. Now you are trying to give it expression. You are trying to comprehend it and accept it—accept the fact that a shift has occurred and you are feeling differently about so many things.

It is now that you must gain a greater experience of Knowledge and recognize that it is a deeper Mind within you, a Mind that is not a product of culture or religion. It is a Mind in the world, but not of the world. It is in stark contrast to your intellect—your social mind that is a product of your social conditioning and adaptation to a changing world.

This deeper Mind is free. It is not subject to manipulation or seduction by the outside world, and that is why it is so very powerful and reliable within you. But it moves mysteriously. It is like the water beneath the ground, moving in a determined fashion but out of sight. Its waters are pure and uncontaminated.

To take the Steps to Knowledge now is to build a connection between your surface, social mind and the deeper Mind of Knowledge within you. For you are beginning to respond to Knowledge, and that is what has created the shift within you. Now you must build a conscious connection so that you can gain a greater awareness and be able to move more effectively with less restraint in the direction that you are really meant to go.

It is in building this connection that you will find the strength and the self-trust and self-acceptance to make real change in your life— not just a cosmetic change, not just a makeover of your current existence, but a real shift in where you live, how you live and who you are with.

In reality, God is calling you, and you must bring yourself into the clear so you can respond and continue to respond as if you are taking now a whole new journey in life.

Perhaps you felt these inclinations previously, but now something has changed, and you have entered a different phase of your life here. You still want a lot of the same old things, but your feelings have changed. Your orientation has changed. Now the deeper needs of the soul are competing with your personal desires, fears and obligations. And you will have to choose again and again, even every day perhaps, which direction you will go, what set of needs are more pressing and important.

This struggle within yourself is very real, and it is particularly intense at certain turning points of your life because now you are going against your social conditioning. You are going against the expectations of others. Perhaps you will have to break some obligations and associations, and you will feel afraid and unsure. And perhaps you will wonder if you are going mad, but you are not going mad. You are just responding to a greater calling. This sets in train a greater momentum and a deeper sense of commitment, but to things unseen and unrecognized. That is why it is mysterious and difficult to explain, and why you cannot explain it to your friends and family.

Only rarely will your friends or family and a special person here be able to recognize and to encourage you, for they recognize the power of freedom and that there is a deeper freedom that certain people must follow. If you have such an ally in life, you are blessed. But you will still have to struggle against all the forces that have been placed upon you by your culture, your family, your religion perhaps, even your nation because it is a struggle for allegiance.

If you are to follow the deeper Intelligence that God has placed within you, then this will create a real change in your allegiance and your attachment and commitment to other things. If you have children, you will still have to raise them, and you may have to take care of aged parents. But beyond this, your first responsibility is to Knowledge, for this is God moving your life.

You must follow this calling without understanding it or being able to explain it even to yourself. It is your ability to do this—which is an ability you build on a daily basis as you take the Steps to Knowledge—that breaks the hold of your social conditioning, breaks the domination of other people and their expectations, frees you from fear and attachment and from obligation to things that no longer represent your greater needs.

In this sense, freedom is not free. It requires a great effort on your part, a growing commitment, a liberation. You cannot follow a greater purpose and have everything else you want in life, for that is trying to move in many directions at once. And that just holds you in place, stuck, as if you were chained to a wall—unable to choose, unable to move, unable to change your circumstances or your agreements with others.

What you need now is stillness, inner listening. You must gain a stronger connection to the deeper current of your life. Instead of it being a fleeting and infrequent moment of experience, you need now to connect with it and to build the connection as if you are building a bridge from one shore to another. And bridges are not built in a day. They require much effort and consistent application.

That is why taking the Steps to Knowledge is so important. You do not do this in leaps and bounds, or your bridge will never be strong or sure. Ultimately, you want to have one foot in this world and one foot in your spiritual reality, knowing that each shore is different, recognizing how much they are different, but how one serves the other in a unique way.

This awareness and education is not the product of speculation but of an aggregate of wisdom based upon experience. It is the foundation of wisdom. It is not an elaborate set of ideas.

Wisdom is like a foundation of stone. Philosophy is like a foundation of sticks. Here the whole creation of your idealism can fall apart with a great shocking experience of life, a great disappointment, a great illness. A building made of sticks can burn up in an hour or collapse under weight or pressure or the movement of the world.

But your foundation in Knowledge is a connection beyond the world. It is deep and profound. It can be shaken and challenged because your allegiance to it is not yet complete or whole, but within itself, it can withstand anything.

It is building your connection to Knowledge that is fundamental. It is allowing questions to be unanswered. It is recognizing the things you know today and abiding with them, but with an open mind.

You build your connection to Knowledge by supporting the things that you really know, and by protecting them from the doubt and accusations of others. For at the outset, you are not strong enough to endure the social pressures and criticism that will be brought to bear upon you if you are indiscreet regarding the deeper experience you are having.

Knowledge holds for you a greater destiny, but first it must have your allegiance. First, you must go through, in stages, a process of reorienting your life and re-evaluating your ideas, your priorities and your values. And this can take quite a bit of time. The longer it takes, the more suffering there is, but in essence it still takes time to go through these stages of reorienting your life.

For now, you are still the same person. You look the same to everyone else. Perhaps you look the same, although you may be acting a little strangely, but really something monumental has happened within you. And now you are trying to deal with it and accept it and follow it.

But it requires that you dismantle much of your old life because you cannot just put a new life on top of an old life. It is more like building a bridge to a new life. But you do not know what that new life is yet. Your connection to the other shore is not strong enough yet. You have not gotten that far yet. Now you are following the impulse to build that bridge, without knowing its ultimate purpose or its ultimate form.

This requires that your mind yield to a greater power. You cannot be in charge of everything, being in control of everything, having everything explained, because you are following a greater power. There must be a yielding here, and perhaps this yielding will occur gradually, incrementally, but there must be a yielding here. At a certain point, you realize that to deny this deeper movement is to deny the essence and meaning of your life, and even if you cannot understand it or control it or define it, you must follow it.

If you do not try to seize it, or do something with it, or give it a form or a definition, then it can lead you safely, with power and stability. But if you try to harness it, to use it, to control it, to stop it, then your life will be in such a state of conflict. And there is no amount of pleasure or personal escape that can relieve you of this conflict. The only way you can overcome this is by following the power and the presence within you.

There will be more thresholds down the way where you will have to choose again because this is a journey with many stages. You only need to attend to the stage you are in. You have not reached certain places along the way. There are more rivers for you to cross, but you are not there yet, so do not concern yourself with that.

Practice stillness. Practice inner listening. Set aside your insecurity and need for answers. Be observant. Be as objective as you can. Look at other people, not with ridicule or condemnation, but see whether their lives are demonstrating a greater Knowledge or not. Whether they be rich or poor, advantaged or disadvantaged, look and see if there is the evidence of Knowledge moving them.

This will give you entirely different criteria upon which to discern the intentions and the reality of other people. And they will teach you dramatically the consequences of living life without this guiding presence within yourself. Their problems, their pursuits, their obsessions, their addictions, their depression, their confusion will all give you great encouragement if you can see their situation objectively, looking for Knowledge.

For in life, there is only Knowledge and the need for Knowledge. That is really all life can show you. There is freedom in this way or subjugation.

When you have made further progress in following the mysterious power of Knowledge within yourself and have allowed your life to go through phases of change, you will look at other people as if they are in chains. Their lives will appear to be slavish and subdued with very little creativity and imagination, a kind of servitude to their ideas, their beliefs and their obligations to others. Even if they are wealthy and can enjoy luxuries, they will look slavish to you, as if they were a group of convicts walking down the road in chains.

This is how the Angelic Presence looks upon the condition of humanity. But they look with compassion, for they are seeking to free those individuals who are ready to be free, who are ready to discover the power and presence of Knowledge within themselves.

And the liberation is not a political liberation or just an escape from unhealthy circumstances. It runs much deeper than this. It is a shift in the authority of your life. Either you are following the social mandates and contracts that have shaped your mind and thoughts and beliefs [or] the mysterious power of Knowledge that is here to initiate you into your greater purpose and into a greater set of relationships in life.

This is a journey and a process. You need strong companions. You need someone to bear witness to what is occurring within you. It is much too difficult to do this alone, particularly if you are under pressure from your friends and family to conform to what they have conformed to. Here you will find much doubt and perhaps discouragement. But every person who has had to break new ground within themselves has had to face this kind of adversity in one way or another.

Find a quiet place where you can practice your inner listening. Practice your Steps to Knowledge because it will teach you how to still your mind and to listen for Knowledge beyond your mind, and how to become used to silence and to recognize silence as the environment for contact within yourself. Instead of just a dark and empty and spooky place, it now becomes a refuge where your mind can be refreshed, your energy can be renewed and your mind can rest. You seek this as comfort and refuge now, not as a duty or a burden or an obligation. And even if your mind is tormenting you in your times of practice, the fact that you are there to pay attention is important.

If you cannot still your mind here, then use your mind to contemplate certain things, important questions. Employ your mind. Do not be its slave. Direct your mind. Do not let it rule you. In your practice, either focus on stillness, using an object or an idea or an image as a focal point for your mind, allowing yourself to sink beneath the surface of the mind. And if you cannot do this, then use your mind to contemplate something important.

Consider, for example, the question of how you can trust and follow Knowledge within yourself, and to what extent would you follow Knowledge? And what circumstances would discourage you, dissuade you or defeat you in this regard?

Here you are giving your mind something useful to think about. Instead of running on and on in all of its anxiety and insecurity, in all of its pursuits and ideas and imaginings, you are giving it something really important to do in service to Spirit, in service to Knowledge.

Ultimately, when you have achieved a higher position on the mountain of life and have gained a greater strength and self-confidence and a greater foundation of wisdom, you will see that the mind should either be still or should be serving a higher purpose. But at that point, Knowledge has become the foundation of your life, and you are operating from a position of Knowledge to a far greater extent than you are doing at this moment.

The needs of the soul are fundamental. You cannot satisfy this with pleasure, with hobbies or distractions, with entertainment, with romance, with sexuality, with intoxication. For the need of the soul is for you to recognize, to experience and to express a greater purpose in life and to adopt the life and the associations that will make this discovery and expression possible. Nothing else will satisfy the deeper need of the soul.

This purpose you create will be in association with certain other people, and perhaps you will only take a supporting role in this purpose that you share. But that is enough. You do not have to be a superstar or a leader or an innovator here. That is very rare.

Your Spiritual Family has sent others into the world who will share your purpose and destiny with you. Some of them will be with you for a lifetime; some for only very brief periods. But you need to find these people, and that represents your deeper searching for relationships. It is not just a need to avoid loneliness or to have companionship or to have friendship or marriage. It is the search for those you are destined to meet. Search for them first. Do not create a life apart from this, or that will all have to be thrown into question once your deeper calling emerges, and that is much more difficult to deal with.

Develop your inner life. Look at your mind objectively. Recognize the degree to which it is controlled by your social conditioning, and how afraid it is of life and of the future.

For the personal mind is based upon insecurity. Born of Separation, it feels it has no real foundation. It has no greater support. It is weak. It identifies with the body, and so it thinks it is mortal and will face endless prospects of loss and deprivation. It is really pathetic until it can serve a greater purpose. And then its real strength, power and capabilities will become discovered and experienced.

As a vehicle of communication, your mind is magnificent. It can do incredible things. But it makes a very poor god. Weak, unstable, prone to extremism, adamant, self-destructive, destructive of others, cruel, dominating, subservient—whatever role it takes, it is born of a fundamental fear and insecurity. Treat it like a child who needs a strong, guiding hand—a loving, guiding hand—and that guiding hand is the power and presence of Knowledge within you.

You may pray fervently to God for guidance and for deliverance, but God has given you Knowledge to guide you, to protect you and to prepare you and lead you to a greater life within the world, within the very circumstances that are emerging now.

This re-establishes your relationship with the world, with God, with your purpose for coming here. Here you begin to see the value of your mind and your body as vehicles of communication. Here you start to understand your unique nature as being appropriate and valuable for the real purpose you are here to serve and to discover.

Here you see your past as a demonstration of life without Knowledge, but you also see in your past that certain skills have been developed, certain talents have shown evidence of their existence. Your past becomes a useful resource now for the cultivation of wisdom, for this foundation of wisdom will give Knowledge within you the greatest avenue of expression.

Instead of your past being filled with regrets, disappointments and self-recrimination, it now becomes a resource for wisdom. And other people's lives become a resource for wisdom. And you seek for this wisdom. You need this wisdom. The greater your foundation in wisdom, the more powerfully Knowledge can communicate through you and the greater your service to others can be. Here you reap the harvest of your life even if it has been difficult.

But you must proceed every day. Carry on your practice every day. Reinforce your allegiance to Knowledge every day. Learn to be tolerant and compassionate of others every day. Learn to be tolerant and compassionate with yourself every day. And hold fast to those things you most deeply know, for they are the bricks of your foundation. And the more you can honor what Knowledge has given you already, the more you will open yourself to what Knowledge has yet to give you and what Knowledge will give you as you proceed.

This is following The Way of Knowledge, a greater journey. Here God will send to you a preparation once you are ready to commit yourself to a spiritual practice. This preparation will not simply be something that tantalizes your mind or ambitions, but something that speaks to your deeper nature powerfully. And others will come into your life who show a greater promise themselves, and they will teach you, through their wisdom and their errors, how to discern and to follow Knowledge within yourself.

As you proceed, you will realize you have a greater destiny here, and it is not a product of your imagination. It is real and powerful and eternal, and it will restore to you your strength and integrity, which were lost to you before.

God has sent you into the world to serve certain people under certain circumstances and to associate with certain people to discover this purpose and to fulfill it. And there will be certain people along the way who will inspire you and will help to point the way so that you do not lose yourself in the world, so that you do not take the wrong turn, for there will be many junctures.

Your allegiance and experience of Knowledge are still very young. It has not grown strong enough to be able to correct every mistake. Even as you become advanced, you realize that the potential for error is still within you, and you will seek for assistance from others who are strong with Knowledge.

You are bringing something rare and extraordinary into the world, something the world cannot itself provide because over this bridge that you have built will come the Power and the Presence of God into the world, and you will be a conduit and a channel for this. And though it may be expressed under very mundane circumstances—by feeding people, taking care of people, helping people, taking care of the environment, assuring the well-being of other species of animals and plants—whatever your specific area of contribution, you are bringing the Power and the Presence into the world, and with it the remembrance for everyone that they too were sent here for a greater purpose, and that it is real and powerful, and it will not abandon them.

May Knowledge grow stronger within you each day. May you take each day as a process of learning about Knowledge and the need for Knowledge. May you put yourself in a position to benefit from your errors and the errors of others, and build your foundation of wisdom, and build your connection to the guiding presence and power in your life. And as you gain confidence and trust and ability, you will be able to give these to others, for the need in the world is immense.

CHAPTER 2

THE FREEDOM JOURNEY

As revealed to
Marshall Vian Summers
on March 2, 2011
in Boulder, Colorado

Spirituality is fundamentally a quest for freedom—freedom from certain things and freedom for certain things.

Seen in this way, the picture becomes more complete. For you have a greater destiny in the world, a greater purpose for being here, a purpose that you are not living now, despite your definitions and proclamations. It is to free you from the life that you are living now to prepare you for a greater life in service to the world that represents the core and essence of all spiritual development.

There are, of course, many other objectives that people bring to their inner life and to their belief in the Divine—pleasing God, having good social standing, being an upstanding member of the religious or church community, following the precepts, being devout [or] being rebellious. Whatever the position may be, you have still not broken free from your previous condition.

You may have wonderful beliefs. You may engage in spiritual practice. You may prostrate yourself at the temple, the church or the mosque. You may go through all the motions of religion and fill your house with religious materials and symbology, but you are not yet free from your previous condition.

This has a great deal to do with both your inner freedom and your outer freedom. You are trying to be free from certain things and for certain things because you have a destiny, because you have a greater purpose.

The struggle for freedom exists at many different levels and represents the core motivation within the individual if they are being honest and faithful to Knowledge within themselves. The struggle for political freedom, the struggle for economic freedom, the struggle for social freedom—the human spirit is not satisfied to be bound and slavish, adhering only to the dictates of culture, politics and religion.

You must see your own motivation for freedom, whatever your circumstances may be, whatever nation you live in, whatever the political climate or the social climate, whether it be tolerant or intolerant, liberal or conservative. Are you living the life you know you must live? That is the question. And the honesty of your answer will be important.

God can provide for you the pathway to take the Steps to Knowledge, the deeper Intelligence within you. But God cannot control what you tell yourself, or what you allow others to tell you, or affect the compromises you make in your own understanding or the compromises you make to acquire things you think you want and need from others.

So the impetus for freedom, the desire for freedom and the certainty that you must claim a greater freedom—all of this must come from you. And it is difficult and challenging. It will threaten your security, your ideas, your complacency, your arrangements with other people. It could challenge your approval that you want from others and your social standing and your position in the family—everything.

But, you see, you are fundamentally in the world to fulfill a greater mission, to prepare yourself for this mission, to free yourself for this mission, to gain the strength, courage and integrity to undertake this mission, to gain the freedom from those things that compromise you and hold you back so that you may have the freedom for the opportunity to engage in a greater life.

If you were to be truly honest with yourself at a deeper level, at the level of Knowledge, this is the truth that you would come upon. But this is a profound truth, far beyond what people think of, consider and tell themselves. People want to be happy. They want to be secure. They want to be comfortable. They want to have companionship. They want to be approved of by others. They want to be liked and appreciated. They want to have pleasures. They want to have comforts.

There is nothing wrong with wanting these things, but you have a greater motivation within you that cannot be compromised for the pursuit of anything else. This represents your first and primary commitment.

If you could query yourself through all of your desires and fears and preferences and needs and assumptions, you would come to this fundamental truth. There is something more important for you to do. You cannot create it. You do not know what it is, but it is there. And you must find a way to find it, to discover it and to express it in the world. This is the core desire, the core intention, the core need— the deeper need of your soul.

Many people, of course, will not go this far with themselves. They want the easy things, the simple things, the pleasant things, the comfortable things. They will not reach very far. They will not question themselves to any great degree. They want comfort and consolation. They do not want to have to work very hard or give up any advantages that they possess or that they think that they must have. So their integrity is lost, and they are strangers to themselves and to the deeper need of the soul.

You see this everywhere, of course. It is the condition of humanity. You see it most tragically portrayed in the more affluent nations where people have gained political freedom and social freedom to a far greater extent than anywhere else on Earth. But they do not use it. They do not claim it. They do not seize upon the great opportunity this gives them. So they seek comforts and pleasures, indulge themselves in romance and hobbies. They try to acquire wealth and lose themselves in their interests and distractions. What a tragic waste this is, that those who have squander what they have, while those who do not have seek it and need it desperately.

That is why the power and the presence of Knowledge is within you. God has given you a deeper Intelligence. It represents the part of you that has never separated from God, and therefore it can be a source of expression of the Creator within you—your connection to the Divine.

Knowledge cannot be fooled. It cannot be seduced. It does not respond to compromise. It is here on a mission, and that mission is your mission. It will not be satisfied with anything else. Even as you meet the basic requirements of life, it will push you further and deeper. It will not let you be satisfied with anything less. Even if you acquire all the things that you think you want and must have, the dissatisfaction will drive you forward. For you must be free for certain things—to meet the people who will be part of your mission, to discover where that mission must be expressed and how it must be expressed.

These are not things that you can figure out in your intellect. It is not an intellectual pursuit. Try as you may to understand it, you cannot unless you take the journey itself. It is a freedom journey.

How far you go on this journey depends upon the level of honesty that you have within yourself. How you express this freedom, how far you take this freedom, depends upon your self-awareness and your honesty within yourself.

Honesty here is so central to the freedom journey. It is so easy to be dishonest, particularly as you gain affluence, as you acquire the comforts that so few people in the world have. The culture will tell you to pursue wealth and happiness and pleasure, marriage and family—everything that you see around you that is being followed and adhered to blindly, often without question. Even the rebels in your society are attached to it, for they have not yet broken free.

People think they know the truth. They think they know what they want because they are trying to use the intellect to determine the purpose, the course and the direction of their lives. But the intellect is a temporary thing, a marvelous instrument it is for communication and evaluation, but it cannot discern the greater truth about your life—why you are here and who sent you. For this, you must go beyond ideas, beliefs and assumptions into a deeper experience.

God has made this possible by placing Knowledge within you. It is not governed by social conditioning. It is not persuaded by the persuasions of the world. It does not bow down to those whom you think you must please and whom you must serve. It is clear. It is compassionate. And it is entirely honest.

Here honesty is not knowing what you feel. It is really feeling what you know. This speaks of a freedom at a greater level—the freedom not only to be safe and secure, the freedom not only to possess advantages in society and comforts. It is a freedom for something greater that pushes you onward, that acknowledges the many things that you have, the many blessings you have and the accomplishments you have made and all the gifts of your society, whatever they may be. But the freedom journey pushes you further.

It is not enough to have. You must know. You must make the deeper connection with Knowledge within yourself. You must begin to live the life you were sent here to live, for nothing else in the world will really satisfy the soul.

Here you must push further. Now you want to become free from things within your own mind—free from fear, free from compromise, free from self-destructive behaviors and attitudes, free from justifications for things that cannot be justified, freedom from appeasing other people, freedom from your own social behavior, which was rarely honest and authentic. You are seeking freedom for a greater engagement within yourself and freedom for a greater engagement in the world, which is calling you as its needs and crises escalate.

This push, this need, this reaching is absolutely natural and essential to you. Yet you will find your friends do not share this. They want to stay behind. They do not want to climb this mountain. They want to be happy. They want to be comfortable. They want to manage what they have already. They do not want to question what they are doing.

They do not want to question their values. They do not want to question what is going on in the world. They are afraid of that! Afraid it might call something greater out of them.

Everyone who is born into the world is on this freedom journey. Yet most people cannot go very far because of oppressive circumstances. Political oppression, extreme poverty, deaden the spirit, deaden the soul. They are struggling to have the simple and basic things of life, and this occupies all of their time and energies.

It is a tragedy of immense proportions, and it is one of the reasons that humanity has not progressed further than it has. For these lives that are meant to be of greater service in the world are being wasted and crushed beneath the weight of poverty and oppression.

For those who have better circumstances, many only want to enrich themselves and insulate themselves from poverty that they see all around them. And the wealthier classes of people, well, their gift and opportunity are so very squandered on empty pursuits, meaningless luxuries and indulgences.

The world offers immense opportunities for people to become lost here. But everyone is still on a freedom journey, even if they have lost their way, even if they have capitulated to their circumstances or to their desires and indulgences. The need of the soul does not change. The direction of Knowledge does not change. The urge for greater freedom, for inner freedom now as well as outer freedom, does not diminish.

This desire, this intention, this will are born of the Fire of Knowledge within yourself. This Fire can become distant and unknown to you, but it does not go out. It is not extinguished, for you cannot extinguish it. You can either become close to it or distance yourself from it. It is either known to you or unknown. You feel it or you do not. You think of it or you do not.

Fundamentally, the expression of a higher purpose is your service to God and to humanity and the world. This transcends your service to yourself or your service to your immediate family. You still provide service for yourself and your family to a certain degree, but the priority shifts to a higher level now.

Yet freedom and honesty still are tied together. There are people who want to serve God and even think they are serving God, but they are not free inside, and they are not really honest with themselves. They think their freedom is serving an ideology or a system of belief, proselytizing that, communicating that, but they are not really free inside. They are driven by personal needs. They are still slaves to the intellect. They have not broken free of the mind. And so their service to God has not really come into being yet, not authentically. It has the appearance of being this, but it is not really there yet. Yet if they become honest with themselves and doubt their beliefs and question their own assumptions, then the pathway to freedom begins to open up for them again.

Then, of course, there are those who are focused only on political freedom or economic freedom or social freedom. This is a very important contribution to many people, and it may be their ultimate purpose to do this, but the question is: Are they free within themselves? Is their motivation based upon love and compassion for people? Or is it driven by anger and hostility, resentment and regret? Is their gift real and authentic, or is it tainted and polluted?

You cannot move another at a deeper level unless you are moved at that level yourself. Those who lead movements of political freedom often become combatants themselves, always at war with the opposition, always trying to overthrow overseeing or overarching powers. They are not free. They are angry. They are desperate. Their hearts are filled with venom.

How can this possibly serve the well-being of people? Even if they provoke a revolution and overthrow the oppressive powers, what kind of government will take its place? Will it be a real social transformation, guided by truly inspired individuals, or will it be a shift in the ruling class alone, a transfer of power from one group to another?

This is why you must look with clear eyes and listen with a quiet mind so that you can hear and see and determine the truth and the authenticity of what you see and hear around you.

It is so easy to have a self-edifying position—to be of service, to sacrifice yourself, to have all the appearances of being a real servant to humanity, a soldier of freedom, a crusader for a greater cause. But what motivates you and what compromises you will make all the difference in the outcome.

You can move people with promises of wealth, freedom and power—social power, economic power, political power. You can move people to do things. You can organize people's activities. But it is the nature of your own motivation that will determine whether you can be a source of inspiration, whether you can ignite the desire for real freedom within others and not merely manipulate people's passions and their oppressive circumstances for your own benefit or gain.

Nations have changed governments at tremendous cost, loss of life and suffering and displacements of people only to find themselves now under a different set of oppressive powers. Was the change really worth it? Was it worth the cost that it required? Have things really improved in the lives of people? Has real freedom been secured?

Look with clear eyes. There must be a greater inspiration to produce a greater outcome. Otherwise, it is all conflict and upheaval, and the condition of humanity has not improved.

You are on a freedom journey. You will not be satisfied with wealth and companionship, pleasure and comfort, if you cannot respond to this within yourself. And it will require you to be free from certain things and free for certain things.

You must have the freedom to open your mind. You must have the freedom to take the Steps to Knowledge and to allow Knowledge to protect you and to guide you towards a greater life. You must have the freedom to be honest with yourself and free from those influences, relationships and circumstances that deny this freedom or make it more difficult to attain.

You must have the freedom to be with yourself completely—facing your limitations, your obstacles, your regrets, your mistakes, your strengths, your weaknesses—everything. You must be free from the fear and avoidance, the habitual avoidance that has denied you access to your deeper nature all these years.

You must have the freedom to be with others and practice a greater neutrality with people so that you may hear them and see them and know them and be able to respond to them at a deeper level, and also to be able to know how to be with them, how to participate, when to participate, when not to participate, what to say, what not to say, what to do, what not to do.

The freedom here is to be guided by Knowledge in all of these matters. You want to be free from those impulses and those fears, those habits and those behaviors that prevent you from really being with people, being open to them, being observant of them, being responsive to them at a deeper level.

Your judgments, your reactions, your unforgiveness, your attitudes, your beliefs—all these things stand in the way of you being present to yourself, to others and to the world. And so you must gain freedom from these things within yourself and within your relationships.

You reclaim the freedom journey by being honest with yourself, by asking yourself, "Am I really living the life I was meant to live?" and not giving yourself the answer you want, but listening more deeply within yourself, and having your most trusted friend and ally respond to this question, and to consider what you tell yourself or the answers you feel that you are being given to this question.

Ask yourself: "Am I where I need to be in life? Am I with the people that I need to associate with? Am I engaged in the activities that are purposeful and necessary for me? Am I using my time well? Should I be in this relationship, and this relationship?"

Review all your relationships, seeking a deeper response from yourself, a deeper honesty, a deeper reckoning. Not playing life for its advantages, but penetrating life for its real truth and direction. Not being a coward. Not being a fool. Not being a slave to the wishes of others or to your own cultural conditioning.

This is honesty. And honesty brings you back to the freedom journey—to the unfinished business of your life, to the core activities and essential pursuits that are before you, and the work that must be done on your inner life and your outer life to bring you closer to the truth of who you are and why you are here.

As you take these steps, you inspire others to take these steps. You strengthen that which is strong, and you weaken that which is weak. Your life becomes a demonstration, which ultimately can be more significant than anything you try to say or do with people.

You have so much more to do and to give than you are doing and giving at this moment, and you know it is true, if you are honest with yourself. The engagement with honesty brings you back to your journey to freedom—freedom from, freedom for, freedom on the inside, freedom on the outside.

Knowledge will guide you to take certain actions. You must be free to take these actions.

Knowledge will reveal certain things to you about yourself and the people around you. You must be free to consider these things and to respond.

Knowledge will take you to certain places. You must be free to go there.

Knowledge will build real relationships with people who have great promise for you. You must be free to participate there.

Knowledge will take you out of situations that are unhealthy or that have no future. You must be free to withdraw.

Knowledge will ask you to wait. You must have the freedom to wait.

Knowledge will require forbearance. You must be able to practice forbearance.

Knowledge will require real discernment and a development of discernment on your part. You must be free to undertake this development.

Knowledge will require that you be discreet and not talk foolishly or mindlessly. You must gain the freedom and the strength to do this.

Knowledge will require that you face the world and the Great Waves of change that are coming to humanity. You must have the freedom and the courage to do this.

All of these freedoms require breaking away from certain things and building other things. They require a thousand little liberations and new beginnings in every aspect of your life.

This is the freedom journey. This is why you have come. You have not come just to put a nametag upon yourself or declare your position in the world. You have come for a greater purpose, and you must be free to find, to discover and to follow this purpose.

God has placed Knowledge within you to make this possible in a world of conflicting and contrasting influences.

Let this be your understanding.

CHAPTER 3

THE PRISON

As revealed to
Marshall Vian Summers
on October 21, 2013
in Boulder, Colorado

You are aware of prisons. They are places where people are incarcerated and neglected and often abused. They are places where people are taken away from normal life and placed under severe limitations and supervision. They are places where people lose contact with the outside world and are often forgotten and overlooked.

Today We speak of the prison within yourself, that which locks you in and holds you back and takes you out of life and separates you from that which you love, that denies you your destiny and your freedom. A prison without walls, without bars, without guards, an invisible prison, the prison in your own mind.

When you look at people, they are there, but they are not really there. They are locked away in their perspective and their attitudes and beliefs; in their grievances, their dreams, their hopes, their fears and anxieties. You speak to them, but they can barely hear you. You look at them, but they cannot really see you. You try to reach them with a gracious message, and they do not know what it is.

They appear to be free in certain nations. They can move about. They can, to a certain degree, determine their occupation, perhaps even have the freedom to choose whom to marry, which is still a rare freedom in the world. But they are still in the prison, you see. It is the prison of Separation, built over time and circumstance, shaping itself and determining what a person can see and not see, do and not do and hear and not hear.

Everyone's prison is a little different, but the reality is still the same. It is your most fundamental problem, beyond acquiring for yourself the basic necessities of life, which for many people is still a grave and urgent need. But once this need has been sufficiently satisfied, and people have a reasonable degree of security in this matter, then they have to deal with gaining a different kind of freedom, a freedom that is not really imposed even from the outside, though it is reinforced there.

It is the prison, you see. You are walled in, kept out. You cannot respond to your Source. Knowledge within you, the deeper Intelligence that God has given you, is giving you signs and clues every day, but you do not hear, you do not feel. And if you do hear, you think it is something else, just another thought in the mind amongst all the other thoughts, which come from nowhere and have no value.

This is the central dilemma, you see, living in Separation, living in the physical reality, living in a body, being circumscribed by a world of constant change and uncertainty, by competition and conflict and the ever-present fear of loss and deprivation. Here the world is not so much the prison, but your mind itself. For you may have all the comforts that money can buy, and yet you are desperate, like a caged animal pacing back and forth, needing constant stimulation, needing constant distraction and obsession that keep you from experiencing your truly miserable state.

THE PRISON

It is only when you realize you are living in this prison, and that you are not living the life you were sent here to live and meant to live, that you begin to turn a fundamental corner in life. It is here that Heaven can truly assist you. But it is a turning with many steps and stages and thresholds. It does not happen all at once in a day or a month or a year. But it must begin with this fundamental need to know your greater purpose in life and to have the inner freedom to experience and to express this.

You can be locked in place in culture and society, economically bound to take care of a family or to function in a role, but you can still have this inner freedom, you see. And if you have this, you become like a saint, like a beacon, a dispenser of wisdom, compassion and forgiveness, someone that people will come to in time to seek advice and resolution because you are the only one amongst them who is really without conflict inside, for you have stepped out of the prison and live there no longer.

In this stage, you are only circumscribed by the limitations of your outer life, but your inner life becomes more boundless, more pure, not beset with constant fear and the constant need to escape from fear that is the fundamental condition of nearly everyone else.

This is a problem for every person, not just those who are elected or those who are the most promising or the wealthiest or have the greatest opportunities. For God has sent every person into the world to serve the world in a unique way with certain people and certain situations. The fact that most people are not engaged in this manner is the cause of suffering at every level, and produces the world that you see and touch and hear every day.

Because of this, it is everyone's problem, central to everyone's core needs. No matter how much people try to satisfy themselves with pleasures and possessions and romance and the quest for power and prestige, this fundamental need lives within them still and cannot be fulfilled in any other way.

They are still in the prison, you see, now more deeply bound by their passions and their pursuits and their ambitions, ever more fearful that they may lose all of these things. Now they have enemies. Now they have competitors. Now they have countless other forces to threaten them. So while they might seem to rise above everyone else in a material sense, they are more aggravated than the average person and will rarely experience a moment of peace and reprieve.

Though this may be the pursuit of the world, Heaven has sent you here for a greater purpose. And only God's New Revelation for the world speaks of this directly. It does not require belief in a great messenger or saint. It does not require adherence to a strict religious philosophy or ideology. It does not require that you belong to a religious system or organization. You may exist within or beyond these things because your fundamental need is beyond these things.

Only God knows how to free you from this prison. You might try any form of escape, trying to live a purely happy, simple life; trying to live a pastoral life; trying to live an agricultural life; trying to build your life in such a way that you do not feel the constant infringement of your inner restraint. But try as you may, spend your lifetime trying to formulate the perfect set of circumstances for yourself, you have not escaped your fundamental problem. And you cannot assure that these circumstances that you have been able to create can be sustained and can be protected, thus giving rise to constant fear and aggravation.

THE PRISON

God understands this predicament because it governs the entire physical universe, a physical universe where the separated must live in countless forms, in countless worlds, in countless expressions of culture and civilization, at countless different levels of technological and social development. It is the condition of living in Separation, in this world and in all worlds where intelligent life has evolved or where it has established a settlement. That is how fundamental this is.

God gave you the freedom to enter Separation, to be an individual, to be alone, to appear to self-determine your life. But this has been your burden as well as your freedom. God understands your predicament, and God has given the answer to the human family and to all families of intelligent life everywhere, in all dimensions and universes. It lives within you today. It is your way out of the jungle. For it is not corrupted. It is not acquiesced. It is not adapted to the world. It does not need approval or reward here. It is without fear, for it cannot be destroyed. It is the only part of you that is pure and fearless, wise and compassionate. It is the part of you that has never left God and is still connected to Creation.

That is why there is no Judgment Day. That is why there is no Hell and damnation because part of you is still living in Creation and cannot be separated from God. But the part of you that has been cast out and has left on your own accord, that is journeying through the physical reality, that is where you are today. But this bespeaks your greater reality, your greater origin, your greater destiny, which exists outside the prison walls of your own beliefs and infringement.

God has the key to your prison gate. And it is perfect. And yet you hesitate because you are not really sure you want to leave the confines of your own mind. Though you suffer there, you also are adapted to this and are afraid of change, thinking that without this confinement, you would be lost. You would be destroyed. You would disappear. But none of this is true. You would still be here. You would still be you. You would look the same in the mirror. Your outer circumstances have not changed. You did not die and go somewhere else.

It is that your mind is opened, and you begin to experience things you never felt before. And you begin to realize you have always had moments of this experience. And you would see this in such contrast to your normal daily state of mind, which is groveling, self-deprecating, fearful and suspicious.

Because you were sent into the world for a greater purpose, you must find the freedom to discover this purpose. You must find the freedom to find those people with whom it is concerned. You must find the courage to undertake the preparation for this. You must build the strength and the self-discipline to travel on a different kind of journey. You must build self-confidence, escaping your self-repudiation and the clouds that hang over you.

Therefore, God's first purpose is to unburden you, to give you the chance to see that your real life is outside this prison, and that you have settled for far too little in life. There is a greater reality awaiting you—a greater calling, a greater purpose, a greater experience of life.

Even if you are bound physically, culturally, bound by poverty and circumstance, your mind then still becomes a conduit for grace. Instead of an individual struggling and striving to survive and to gain happiness from whatever can be acquired, you now become a portal through which Heaven can speak and shine upon the world, a world that is growing darker with each passing day, a world that is facing the Great Waves of change.

THE PRISON

Without this power and this grace, you will become ever more fearful and discontented as the world around you changes and becomes more difficult. You will become ever more affected by people who are now becoming more angry, more judgmental, more threatened by the great change that is occurring throughout the world. You will become more isolated. You would feel that your survival and your affluence and your well-being are under constant attack. You would blame others for this, perhaps even whole nations of people that you do not even know. You would become partisan. You would be conflicted. You would be at war with yourself, caught up in wars occurring all over the world.

But God has sent you here for a greater plan and a greater purpose, not to fall into this hellish trap, not to descend into chaos and misery in the prison house of your own mind, but to allow your mind, this beautiful instrument of communication, to be a medium through which greater gifts can be given to the world through you, for which you were perfectly designed.

This then is how God will redeem you and restore you—not because you have assumed a preferred belief; not because you have believed in the Jesus, the Buddha or the Muhammad, but because you have opened to the power of Knowledge that God has placed within you. Here Jesus, the Buddha and the Muhammad become examples of contribution, of freedom in the greatest possible ways.

Though you are not asked to do what they did, you are in essence undergoing the same process of preparation. But this must be a conscious journey. Do not think that you are on this journey already and that you are making great progress. Until your internal state begins to change, your values begin to change, your priorities begin to change, the nature of your inner experience begins to change, then you are not really set on this journey yet. Perhaps you are standing on the shore, looking at the great ocean before you and wondering what is on the other side.

God's first purpose is to unburden you, which is giving you escape from your prison because within your prison, you cannot see, you cannot know, and you cannot hear sufficiently to recognize the greater journey that is yours to take. You are far too confined within yourself and subject to the influence of other people that are oppressing you to be able to have the strength and the determination to set out.

On this journey, you do not necessarily leave your family or circumstances, for in many cases this is not possible or even appropriate. This is an internal journey, the greatest you will ever take, the most profound, for it is the Will of Heaven that you do this—fundamentally, essentially, beyond all of the beliefs and perspectives, beyond religion, beyond nationality, beyond race and tribe, culture and custom.

This is your contract with God. This is what has brought you into this world with a greater purpose. And this is what will restore you here, for you must be here to be restored in this way.

You may pray. You may fall down on your knees. You may recite the sacred texts. You might try to live perfectly, according to the prescription of religion. While this is a noble enterprise, it does not guarantee your escape from the prison.

For many people, this even deepens their incarceration. Now they become vehement about their beliefs and judgmental of everyone else. Now they think their beliefs are the only or most important beliefs that everyone should believe and that those who will not and cannot believe should be punished or cast out or even destroyed. They have turned God's great Revelation now into a weapon, to be used for power and condemnation.

This is trying to believe inside your prison. This is what it looks like if you do not find escape and relief from your confinement internally.

It is unnatural to be incarcerated. You were not designed for this. It is unnatural to be bound so tightly, restrained so much by your culture and your own inner beliefs and emotional states. It is unnatural to base your life on ideology alone, for in your natural state, you do not have ideology. You do not need ideology. While you are in this world, in your natural state, you need a framework in which to work, but you see that God moves in and beyond all things. Flowing like the wind through the forest trees, it is not bound there, though it lives there as well.

Therefore, seek escape from your prison. Recognize your prison. Become aware of your own inner states and attitudes as objectively as you can, and you will see how restrained you are, how obsessed you are, how depressed and repressed you are—not only by outside forces and circumstances, but your own inner states.

You cannot change your outer circumstances to make everything perfectly agreeable without becoming self-deceptive or delusional. But you can open the prison gates of your mind, and God has provided the Steps to Knowledge to make this possible. God has provided the way out—not just something to believe in, not just guidelines for personal behavior, not just commandments for living in the world, but the actual pathway out of your prison house, out of the fog of confusion and self-repudiation.

Everything that is destructive in the human mind, the source of all destructive behavior, the source of all cruelty, the source of all violence and grievance is confusion. And confusion is the product of being unnatural. It is an unnatural condition. Where you have come from and what you will return to is not a state of confusion, but of great certainty and humility.

Therefore, do not try to figure out how you are going to be happy in life. Certainly, there are problems to solve and dilemmas to address. Certainly, there are corrections to be made that you can see even today. But you do not know the way out of this jungle, for you do not have the key to your prison.

But God is providing the key, once again. This time it is being given in a pure form, being recorded for the first time in all of human history in its pure form—so pure you can even hear Our Voice, the Voice that spoke to the Jesus, the Buddha and the Muhammad. You can hear. You can read. You can understand—because this is the Voice of Heaven speaking to you. And its first purpose is to give you freedom—not complete freedom because that is not fully possible here, but the freedom to find and to discern the deeper voice that God has placed within you and to follow that voice and to allow it to reshape your thinking and your life.

There is no one in the world who could figure out how to make this work, though people keep trying. God is giving you, then, a pathway out. It is not filled with grandeur and miracles and promises of ecstasy. It is just the pathway out. It restores to you the primary connection between your worldly mind and the deeper Mind of Knowledge within you. And through this connection, you are given things to do that are really restorative, that bring resolution to your life, that counteract the forces and tendencies within your mind that deepen your prison and keep you trapped there.

What a blessing, then, to live at a time of Revelation, when such a gift is available to you in the purest possible form, living at a time when God's new Messenger is in the world, bringing this Revelation to as many people as possible. You are blessed to hear this and to receive this.

God has attempted this before, but God's Revelations have been miscast and misunderstood, misused, and turned into a form of oppression, a yoke for the people.

Only those who have a greater sense of Heaven can see beyond these things and use the great traditions beneficially. But this requires a deeper sense. You must be thinking outside the prison to feel these things—to feel this greater association; to have a sense that you are being watched over, beneficially, with great wisdom and compassion; to see that your sins, however deep, cannot prevent you from receiving the Grace of Heaven.

The goal here is not to escape the world or die and go to some heavenly state, but to become what you are really meant to become here, in whatever circumstances you find yourself, whether you are rich or poor, whether you are free to travel or not free to travel.

Whether you can alter your circumstances or not alter your circumstances, you become a light in the world because you are free of the prison—free enough to live outside of it, to see the stars beyond the clouds, to witness the beauty of nature at every moment, to marvel at life's thousand simple pleasures, to feel the presence of Heaven blessing you so that you may have the power and the opportunity to bless others with that which is pure and beyond definition.

CHAPTER 4

THE REVOLUTION

As revealed to
Marshall Vian Summers
on May 24, 2011
in Boulder, Colorado

You were born with two minds, the Mind that God created and the mind that has been shaped and conditioned by the world, your worldly mind. At this moment, you have these two minds.

The worldly mind you are probably very familiar with since it dominates you almost a hundred percent of the time. That does not mean you are fully aware of it or all of its thoughts and impulses, for people are very afraid to go to experience certain parts of their worldly mind—the dark and fearful parts, the dangerous parts, the mysterious parts.

People keep striving into the future, in part to run away from their current experience, and that is why most people cannot sit still for five minutes. They are afraid of their own mind, the worldly mind.

Yet there is a deeper Mind within you, the Mind We call Knowledge. It represents the part of you that has never left God. It is not religious because when you are connected to God, there is no need for religion. Religion does not make any sense. There is just reality. But this is a deeper and greater reality than the reality that you experience in your worldly mind.

So you have these two minds. They are so very different. One is far more powerful than the other. The purpose of all spiritual practice is to bring you to the deeper Mind. It is not merely to have faith in God, or faith in the prophets, or faith in one's beliefs and religious principles.

The real purpose of spiritual practice is to bring you to the deeper Mind, to connect your worldly mind to the deeper Mind. For the deeper Mind cannot serve your worldly mind, and your worldly mind must serve the deeper Mind.

It is only here that you find true integrity. It is only here that you are fully yourself. It is only here that you find your greater strength, purpose and destiny. It is only at this level that you can truly discern relationships and know who to be with and how to be with them, regardless of other attractions or inducements. There is no greater value or reward in the world, or in any world in the universe, than to reconnect with the deeper Mind.

This deeper Mind calls to you. It has the attraction of the Divine. It is where you connect with the Divine. It is where God's Will communicates to you, not in words but in impulses, at a deeper level—beyond the realm of the five senses, beyond the realm of the intellect, beyond the realm of ideas and ideology.

This is the Great Attraction. But people are afraid, and so they stay busy and occupied. They stay obsessed with things on the outside, pursuing a whole host of things, most of which can never be fulfilling—full of fear, full of ambition, full of grievance, full of fantasy. This is what dominates your worldly mind.

THE REVOLUTION

Work here becomes not merely useful and important, but actually obsessive and distracting. For if you cannot be with yourself for five minutes, how can you be with anyone, really? How can you be with anything? How can you be creative? How can you be insightful? How can you be reflective and aware of your errors?

People know they are weak and fallible, but they try to reinforce their beliefs as a show of strength, a great show of strength. The firm belief, the committed believer, is like a block of concrete—unresponsive, dead, immovable, resistant, disconnected, defensive, judgmental. This is the personal mind in a state of retreat and solidification. It is a prison without walls, but so fixed that nothing can move it.

You are bound to things you cannot even see, bound by fear—the fear of being wrong, the fear of being lost, the fear of having made a mistake in your life and facing that, the fear of wasting your life and having to face that.

What is pride but fear masquerading as something else? What is self-assurance but insecurity parading as something else?

To begin to respond to your deeper nature, to the greater Mind within you, begins a revolution—a revolution where the existing and former powers are overthrown, gradually, and even through periods of struggle, [by] something far more potent and real and meaningful.

Ideologies are overthrown. Former associations are overthrown. Self-repudiation is overthrown. The gods of your former life are shown to be false and weak, and in time they are overthrown. Your religious principles prove to be too limited and cannot speak to the mystery of your life, and even they can be overthrown. Even things that were useful to you and brought you to the revolution, even they prove to be unnecessary now. You cannot rely upon them.

People come to God's New Revelation, or even to God's former Revelations, seeking peace and comfort, but if they are really serious about their engagement, then it begins a kind of revolution, which is not very peaceful, not very comforting. All Hell breaks loose on the road to Heaven.

The truth is within you, but you must pass through the mind to get there. And the mind is full of many things—things you are not even yet aware of, demons of your own creation, demons of other people's creations—all phantoms in the night. They appear so formidable, you are afraid to approach them. But they are mere phantoms.

In the process of taking the Steps to Knowledge, you have wonderful moments of reprieve and recognition, and you have other times when you are really struggling, struggling because you have to choose something other than what you formerly believed in.

You see the outcome of a relationship before you begin it, and you have to accept this. You begin to see the truth in things, and that conflicts with what you want from them. You start to see that your former goals are not really in keeping with your greater destiny, and so you must have the strength to set them aside. You feel called to go to certain places, and you must have the strength and the freedom to go to these places. You must break the chains of obligation to certain people and situations that are not part of your greater life. You must have the strength to do this.

This strength, this freedom, this determination, this self-honesty all come from Knowledge, for Knowledge is free. Knowledge is honest. Knowledge is determined. Knowledge is powerful.

It is so much in contrast to your worldly mind, which has none of these qualities, in truth. It is weak. It is deluded. It is pathetic. It is groveling. It is self-condemning and condemning of others. It is weak. It is vengeful. It is obsessive.

In reality, your worldly mind is meant to serve Knowledge. Here its greater strengths and intelligence and capabilities become really utilized, and it is redeemed and given a greater purpose and integration into your life.

But before this can happen, there must be a revolution—a spiritual revolution, a revolution against ideas and obligations, against fear, against guilt, against obsession, against grievances—a revolution to free you to find that which is calling to you and which has been waiting for you for so long.

Here you find that being with Knowledge is entirely different from being lost in your thoughts, and you find that people are not present to themselves or each other because they are lost in their thoughts. Here you find that the truth is like the sun, and thoughts are like the clouds that obscure it. Here you find that Knowledge is strong and permanent—it does not change from day to day—and that this is in contrast to your worldly mind, which is always in a state of flux and confusion despite its proclamations of certainty and self-assurance.

That which is weak within you must serve that which is strong. Knowledge cannot and will not serve your worldly mind. It is far more powerful than your worldly mind. It is not afraid of the world.

It is not afraid of death. It is not afraid of loss. Can you claim to have this fearlessness for yourself? In all honesty, you cannot.

That which is weak becomes redeemed serving that which is strong. The part of your mind that is weak becomes redeemed serving the part of you that is strong. The body is weak, but it becomes renewed and strengthened by serving something greater.

God does not condemn you. God is not interested in your pathology, obsessions or distractions. God is just calling you, through the presence of Knowledge within yourself and the presence of Knowledge in those whom you might encounter, which is strong enough to reach through your distractions and preoccupations to actually gain your attention. This is when people have inspiring moments, moments of prescience, moments of recognition, moments of insight, moments of certainty.

God's New Revelation has provided the Steps to Knowledge, and there are many of them. Part of their purpose is to orient your worldly mind to think in harmony with your deeper Mind so that the revolution can be easier, and the transition more smooth and more fluid and more expedient.

It [Steps to Knowledge] provides a contrast between the state of Knowledge and your worldly state of mind so that you can look upon your worldly state more objectively, more compassionately, with greater kindness and acceptance. For Knowledge is not condemning you. It is only calling for you. And the pull of the Divine is so powerful once you begin to feel it, accept it and allow it to be in your experience.

THE REVOLUTION

But in times of struggle, it will seem like you are at war with yourself. A great battle is raging over who will have predominance—your personal mind resisting, trying to lose itself again in its romances, its pursuits, its acquisitions, its obsessive work ethic, its religious ideology, its political campaigns, all of these things pulling you away, away, away—away from the pull and the presence of Knowledge within you.

As you proceed and become wiser, you will be able to recognize the struggle and realize that it is part of the learning process because all learning requires unlearning. All learning requires overcoming previous notions, beliefs, assumptions and ideas. All real learning is rethinking, re-evaluating and reapplying what you know in your life. Learning here is not simply to pass tests or to recite things in the moment as they are called for. This is real education—pure, powerful, redemptive, constructive and potent.

Any real learning situation is like a revolution. It requires you to be more present, to pay attention, to wake up from your dreaming state, to overcome that which has been ruling your life previously—the false rulers of belief, ideology, obsession, fear and fantasy.

You see in the world around you revolutions against oppressive rulers when people can no longer stand the restrictions, the corruption and the brutality that oversee their life and conditions, and they are willing to risk everything to make a change possible.

You who have been living already with things you know you must do that you are not doing, you must reach this point of no return with yourself, where you cannot stand the oppressive nature of your mind any longer. You cannot stand the way you are with people or the way you are with yourself any longer, and so the revolution begins.

But the revolution must have a real goal. It must be freedom for something and not merely freedom from something. And this is where the Revelation gives you a very clear objective. This is why Knowledge redeems you, because it is your goal.

The mind works in harmony when it is serving something greater. But what it serves must be real, beneficial, authentic. It must be greater. It must be real. Your revolution cannot simply be to overthrow a former power. It must be to establish a new state of being.

You can change your outer life endlessly, traveling about, always having new experiences. But We are talking about the revolution within—the thing that people will not face, the thing that people will not attend to, the thing that people will avoid, endlessly seeking that which has failed them so many times before.

The real revolution will not be sparked by grievance and anger but really by a deeper calling that has no anger, that has no grievance. It is this that sparks the revolution within. For that which is gracious and powerful stands in marked contrast to that which is not. And you cannot have them both. One must lead. The other must follow. Knowledge will not follow. It will only recede if it is not being honored and recognized.

Therefore, your choice is very limited, and that is good because that gives you a clear pathway without ambiguity, minimizing the risk of misunderstanding and misperception.

This is taught in all the religions, but the religions have been changed, overlaid with ritual and ceremony, ideology and interpretation. It would take a wise teacher within any one of them to bring you to this pure pathway.

God's New Revelation is unencumbered by all of these things. It presents the Steps to Knowledge very clearly. It is a new hope for a struggling and declining humanity.

Accept the revolution. Be a revolutionary in this way, only. Allow the revolution to be stimulated by something great, powerful and gracious. See yourself going through it. Allow it to happen. Accept it. Keep moving forward. Realize that change is not peaceful. It is challenging and uncertain. It can be very uncomfortable at moments, at times. Accept this and move forward.

You must get up this mountain so you can see. Do not stop long for anyone or anything, and the battle will be over. Your way will be smoother. There will be problems. There will be issues. There will be temptations from the world. There will be old habits that can re-emerge, but once you become strong with Knowledge, none of these things can really hold you back any longer.

You have a greater calling in the world. You must prepare before you can know what this is. You must go through a revolution before you can be in a position to accept a greater responsibility and awareness in life. You must be anchored in Knowledge so that you will have the courage, the clarity and the self-honesty to assume a greater role and a greater service in the world.

Under the old rulers, this is not possible. And so there must be a revolution, a revolution within, a revolution in your thinking and in how you relate to others and to the whole world.

CHAPTER 5

THE TURNING POINT

As revealed to
Marshall Vian Summers
on January 24, 2013
in Boulder, Colorado

Once you begin to become really honest with yourself about your life and affairs, no matter how painful this recognition might be in the moment, it marks a turning point in your life—a turning point where you begin to see things more clearly and are more willing to see things more clearly, to be more honest with yourself about your engagements with people and about your plans and goals, and even eventually about your fundamental beliefs, which are rarely questioned honestly.

This turning point is born of suffering. It is born of the recognition that you are failing in your attempt to organize your life successfully in keeping with how you really feel on the inside. Perhaps it [your life] meets the criteria of culture and the expectations of your family and others, and they hail you as a success, but inside there is emptiness. Inside, you know you have not found solid ground. You have not reached that which you are searching for.

Even if you were to acquire all things representing success and advancement in this world—beautiful relationships, lovely family, beautiful home—even if your work was meaningful in some way, which is so seldom the case, if you are not finding that which is your purpose, your soul will be starving. You will be suffering on the inside. You will congratulate yourself and allow others to

57

congratulate you, but on the inside, you are frightened and unfulfilled.

This is the turning point, you see. You are tired of suffering, tired of false ideals, tired of striving for that which cannot satisfy you. Perhaps in a moment of despair or extreme self-doubt, you begin to ask yourself, "What is the truth?" You ask it now not to parlay with the truth, not to negotiate with the truth, but simply because you need it with your heart and soul.

This marks the turning point and begins the return. At the outset, the return may not be evident at all. You are simply questioning now. You are doubting things you believed in before. You are doubting the values you grew up with, the values that may be expected of you to adopt and to fulfill. But you are beginning, perhaps in the very slightest way, your return to your Source, your return to the greater purpose that has brought you into the world, which has been unaccounted for in your previous efforts and associations.

You do not know what this is, for you have not reached the place where you can see it clearly. For you are in the stage of undoing, the stage of dismantling what you have created that is not true, that is not authentic, that does not represent your heart and soul. You built these things out of convenience, or expediency, or pressured by the expectations of others, or the belief you could only be happy and have meaningful relationships if you acquired such things and such status.

Now the clouds have gathered around your dreams, your hopes and your fantasies, and you find yourself in a state of despair, a state of frustration and anxiety. Perhaps you think you are failing in life, but Heaven looks upon this as a great and hopeful sign.

Perhaps now there is a chance, a distant chance but a real chance, that this individual may turn this corner and continue to bring real honesty to their endeavors and have the courage to release those things that are untrue or inappropriate.

It is in this process of undoing that you gain your connection to Knowledge, the deeper power within you that God has given you to guide you, to protect you and to lead you to a greater life of contribution and fulfillment in the world.

Perhaps this journey will be long with many stages. You cannot control the process. You can only accelerate it by bringing this greater honesty to your mind and your thoughts and your engagements with others.

It is very important at this turning point not to discuss this with people who cannot understand, not to discuss it with your friends and companions, who may have no capacity to realize what you are going through. More than likely, they will attempt to encourage you to keep going with what you were doing before and not to fall prey to self-doubt, not to fall prey to the persuasions of others.

Here you will see who the real advocates for freedom really are in your life. And though they may be well meaning and have a regard for you, if they cannot understand what you are experiencing truly, then they can be a great hindrance to your progress.

You come upon this turning point not only by discovering the emptiness of your rewards or the failure of your pursuits, but also because Heaven is calling you. The time for you to begin the return has come, and now there is another force in your life—a mysterious force that you cannot understand with the intellect, a force you cannot bargain with, a force that will become stronger as you proceed. Now it is a faint light in your mind, but it is a light, and it is casting its revelation upon your life as it truly is, and you are having to deal with the consequence of this.

You may feel you have failed in all ways at this time, but for Heaven this is the beginning of a new life, a life of true promise, true accomplishment and genuine and greater relationships. Now you are beginning the return. But to begin, you must release yourself enough from your former engagements to have the clarity of mind to be free of the influences that were so persuasive over you before—influences you barely understood, but which had great impact on your thinking and behavior.

You need time, time to reconsider, time to build enough courage within yourself to honor your own integrity, which had been lost before and which you must regain now—step by step, event by event, decision by decision. Now your journey is one of unraveling the chains that held you back, undoing that which could not lead you to your real life—facing the betrayal of yourself and your dishonesty with others, facing the pain, but also feeling the rightness and the correctness of what you are now just beginning to contemplate.

Yes, there is pain here, but it is the pain of redemption. It is not the pain of being lost in the world, a casualty of the world, a slave of the world.

You will have to make decisions now, very simple decisions, one by one. You cannot remake your life, for that is not the purpose of this at this moment. It is to free yourself. It is to undo the knots that tie and have held you down. It is to correct the understanding with certain people to whom you have pledged yourself before you had an idea or an understanding of your real nature and purpose in the world.

Your return will be rocky. It will be turbulent. It will be uncertain. You will find yourself falling backwards, having to pick yourself up and choose again. You will see the power of persuasion now in a clearer light. The more you can experience this desire for the truth, the more it will show you in contrast all the decisions that you have made, all the agreements you have made, all the alliances you have established that stand in great contrast to a deeper feeling and recognition within yourself.

Here you must ask yourself, "Am I living the life I was meant to live?" You must ask this continuously, you see, because it will remind you that you are undergoing a great and profound change—a change beyond the realm of the intellect, beyond your intellectual capacity, beyond your manipulation and control. Allow this change to continue.

Heaven is pulling you now. The light within you is growing a little stronger every time you choose to follow the truth. Even if it means starting your life anew—with no friends, no recognition, no promise of success and advancement—if this is what is required, then you must follow this.

This is the birth of real freedom, inner freedom—the freedom to be truly honest with yourself, the freedom to recognize the truth, the truth that seems to escape all others who want to manipulate their life for their own designs.

Here you are pulled out of the crowd and set on a greater journey, but at this point you know nothing of the end point or the result. You do not know what it will lead to, or what it will mean, or who it will bring into your life.

If you are married with children, it all depends on what Knowledge requires you to do. Certainly, you are responsible for the raising of your children and their support, but if your marriage is not in harmony with the birth of the revelation within you, then you will have to follow Knowledge to know what to do and how to proceed.

This can be very challenging. It is as if you have to pass over the greater threshold at the outset just to be able to begin. For you are embarking on a new life, and your spouse may not want to go with you or be able to go with you. And in fact they may be in grave doubt and consternation over the change that is occurring within you. You are threatening your establishment with them. You are threatening your allegiance to them. This can give great rise to anxiety in their mind. But the Power of Heaven is greater than the obligations of Earth.

Here you must follow step by step. Here the truth will become ever more apparent whether your partner can go forward with you in this greater journey or not. You will not be able to explain yourself for a while, for you have not gained enough understanding of your journey to tell other people what you are really doing. What you can say is, "I am following a deeper strength and certainty within myself, and I must follow this. I must understand what it means for my life and where it might lead me."

The return can be very difficult under these circumstances, but difficulty means that the decisions you make will have greater impact and greater significance, and will provide strength and wisdom to you to a far greater degree than if your decisions were far smaller and less challenging.

Heaven knows the return. Heaven is orchestrating the return. But it is you who must make the decisions and the adjustments and deal with the consequences. So do not think you are a blind follower. Do not take a passive attitude. Do not think that you will just be guided in all things, as if you were a little child.

You must make the decisions. You must face the consequences. You must speak for yourself. Therefore, let the mystery of your engagement with Heaven remain a mystery to those around you. Unless they can comprehend deeper things of this nature, this should not be mentioned or discussed.

You must make your decisions and be responsible for them. To do this, you will develop the courage, the strength and the determination to carry forward, which would not be cultivated if you were just a blind follower or thinking that you are going to be guided in all things.

As you will see over the process of the return, those who guide you have others to care for, and they cannot abide with you at all times. It is the strength of Knowledge within you that will respond and that will be your strength, that will be your foundation, that will give you the courage to proceed when everyone around you is in doubt.

That is why you take the Steps to Knowledge. At some point, you must begin the actual preparation because only here can you develop day by day the strength and the connection you will need to be able to receive correction and directives from the Higher Powers, from the Angelic Assembly. But before they can truly direct you, you must have this strength and this courage. In this, you must prove yourself, you see. You must prove yourself to them and to yourself that you have courage and can be trusted and counted upon to do greater things—things beyond your understanding, things beyond your fears and preferences. This is what it means to live a greater life.

Once you are on the return, it is important that you find the correct companions, the correct understanding, the correct preparation and eventually the correct teacher. Here you can become lost once again, for there are many voices. There are many doors. There are many promises. That is why Knowledge within you is the absolute fundamental power, for it will seek only that which is true and forego all other offers, opportunities and inducements.

Here your journey must be strengthened and accelerated, for time is of the essence. You do not have a lot of time. Even the world does not have a lot of time. You have many things to prepare for. Your life must be brought into balance and correct focus and engagement.

The more you hold back, the more you will suffer and be lost in indecision and ambivalence. Here it is better to forge ahead without knowing the outcome than it is to linger, hoping to carry with you the benefits you enjoyed before. For that will only lead to greater aggravation, suffering and misery for you and greater experiences of failure and disappointment.

Therefore, do not think you have all the time in the world. Do not think you can take your time. Do not think that it is not important what you choose to do and how you involve yourself.

Heaven is calling you. It is for a greater purpose. It is for the very purpose that has brought you into the world. It is for the very thing you have been searching for hopelessly in all of your previous endeavors.

God's New Revelation in the world can prepare you, for it is without human corruption. It is without human commentary. It is without the weight of history, human conflict and misunderstanding.

Here the Steps to Knowledge are provided in the clearest possible terms. They are challenging because you must be engaged. You do not want your mind to be drifting in a fog of confusion and anxiety. You want to bring it into the engagement as strongly as possible. You do not want your preparation for your greater life to be halfhearted or based upon ambivalence or confusion.

Therefore, once you set out, you must really set out. You must become determined. Certain things will prove to be false. Certain promises and expectations will prove to be untrue. You must face these things. It is all part of your essential education, you see.

To recognize the true, you must recognize the false. To feel what is true, you must feel what is false. To hold to what is true, you must recognize the persuasions and the inducements of the false. This you gain over time. This is called building wisdom.

Here your errors and mistakes and the regrettable things from your past become the real ground for developing true wisdom, for they all demonstrate the need for Knowledge. They all prove to you beyond a shadow of a doubt that you cannot return to those things, and knowing what not to do then brings greater clarity and focus to what must be done.

For you have a path and a journey to follow. It has a certain direction. It has certain goals and thresholds. It is not about wandering aimlessly in the world. It is not about being free to be whatever you want or do whatever you want without consequence, for that is merely chaos.

Here Knowledge grows stronger because it is the Power of Heaven within you. This is your connection to God. This is where the Light of Heaven is shining deep within you. You return here every day. Under all circumstances attempt the return, and this will grow stronger—giving you its certainty, its power and its direction and the ability to discern the true from the false in ways you could not do before.

Here your studenthood must be determined and not merely casual. If it is casual, it means you are still ambivalent. You have not yet found the ground of your certainty sufficiently to give you the determination you will need to create and follow a new life, guided now by the Greater Powers and confirmed by Knowledge within yourself.

Here you end the Separation within yourself between your worldly mind and the deeper Mind of Knowledge within you. Here your soul regains its connection to Heaven. Here true happiness and genuine relationships can be established. Here your true promise in the world becomes possible, where it was not possible before.

It is not a matter of having choices. It is a matter of knowing what to follow within yourself. It is not the matter of being free to do whatever you want. It is the matter of being free to do what you truly know to do. That is the real meaning of freedom.

Here everything you believed in before, which seemed so noble and valuable and edifying in your earlier life, now are redefined, for now they have a true context and a true meaning. Freedom, redemption, relationship, contribution, dignity, purpose, meaning, service—all these things now begin to have a very true meaning because their context is being established. Whereas before they were merely ideas, beliefs, hopes and wishes, now they become the foundation of your life, not because of what you believe in, but because of how you live and what you do.

This is the return. It has different thresholds, for there are things you must learn and unlearn along the way, things you are not even ready for at this moment.

You are still halfhearted in your approach. You let your mind wander constantly. You still engage in small activities that confuse you and lead you astray. You still give yourself the right to do certain things that are harmful to you, with lots of excuses and explanations. You still indulge in self-doubt, self-pity and self-condemnation. You still judge others habitually, condemning them for their failures, condemning the world for not being what you want it to be, being upset over little things, being preoccupied over little things, being obsessive about yourself and others.

There are many thresholds yet to come where you have an opportunity to recognize these things and to free yourself from them. For it is all about freedom, you see—the freedom to see, the freedom to know and the freedom to act with the power of Knowledge within yourself.

Here you will find that restraint will be so very necessary and will be one of the first things you must really learn to recognize and to employ. For you cannot give yourself away as you did before. You cannot allow yourself to become involved in social engagements like you did before. You will have to hold yourself back. You will have to hold back your speech. You will have to hold back your judgments and condemnation. You will have to restrain yourself from making obligations that are improper. You will have to hold yourself back from trying to have things you want which are not good for you, which will only waste your time and your life even further.

Here restraint is protecting you. It is taking away the freedom that was chaos and giving you the freedom that is true. It is teaching you to be strong with yourself, teaching you how to manage your mind and thoughts, how to not be a victim or a slave to your desires or compulsions.

This is all returning strength, power and determination to you and the courage to face things that other people will not face, to take a course of action that few around you are taking, to free yourself from having to have agreement and approval and consensus.

It is a great freedom, but it must be hard won. At times you must do battle with yourself. For part of you wants to go back to what is safe and secure, that which has no challenge. Part of you lives back there still. But the greater part of you must go forward. And the part of you that is small and weak must learn to follow that which is strong and certain. This is the return.

The return to God is not leaving the world. It is coming into the world to understand the world, to understand yourself in the world and to follow that which is guiding you to give your specific gifts where they are truly needed, which is something the intellect can never really determine.

Your work is here. You will return to your Ancient Home in time, but your work is here. If it is being truly approached, if it is being truly recognized, it will give you power, certainty and great strength in the world. If it is not being approached, then you are lost in a sea of confusion, self-doubt, frustration and disappointment.

And there is nothing that can really save you except coming to terms with your own integrity, except coming to terms with the truth of your life, which begins the return—the return to that which you came here to do, the return to your true integrity, the return to the strength and power you had before you came into the world, which was lost in the maze of confusion, frustration and influence in your earlier life.

Blessed is the return, but it can be very challenging at times. However, the suffering this might entail is nothing compared to the suffering that will be felt increasingly as you age, as the promise of your life becomes ever more distant, as you have to live with the consequences of your poor decisions and the aggravation this creates within yourself.

The question is not about being at peace and being happy. The question is about living the true life. This will give you inner peace. This will give you true happiness, but it is challenging in and of itself. You do not have it by merely wanting it. You must take the journey, the journey of many steps.

This is the true promise of your life. You earn back your strength. You earn back your dignity. You earn back your discernment and discretion. You earn back the power to make true decisions. You earn back the power to free yourself from divisive or destructive engagements. You earn the power to see what is true and what is untrue, and the discernment you will need with others to see what is true and untrue within them. You must regain this. It is there for you to reclaim.

CHAPTER 6

THE GIFT OF A NEW LIFE

As revealed to
Marshall Vian Summers
on May 14, 2011
in Boulder, Colorado

God's New Revelation is not here to simply add value to your current existence or to validate your current ideas and pursuits. It is not here to validate the world's religions or to conform to their beliefs or expectations, for God is not bound by these things. It is not here to validate your expectations, for the Creator of all the universes is certainly not bound by this.

Really, the New Message from God is here to provide a new life for those who can truly respond to it, to give them a greater foundation upon which to build a meaningful life—an inspired life, a life that is guided by Knowledge, a life of true relationships and meaningful engagement with the world.

Here roles are not assigned, but people are given the foundation so that Knowledge within them, the greater power that God has given to guide them, may become evident to them, that they may learn through time to trust this and to follow this, navigating the difficulties of life and the greater difficulties they will have to face in a new world of diminishing resources and greater instability.

People come to the New Message to see if it conforms to their beliefs, their ideas and their expectations. Of course, it does not do this. People come to the New Message from God wanting to use it as a resource to get what they want for themselves. But the New Revelation has a greater plan and promise for them.

People come to the New Message hoping that they will find the wisdom necessary to correct their mistakes and to make their current investments profitable and meaningful. But the New Message is here to give them a new life—not simply a new idea put upon an old life, not simply a sweetener to make the bitter taste of their current experience more palatable and acceptable. People expect too little and want too little, and their expectations are not in keeping with the meaning and the power of the Revelation.

People come to God's New Revelation wanting to see how they can use it right away, as if it is nothing more than a series of tools that people could use to try to improve their lives. But they cannot improve their lives because they do not know what they are doing. They do not know where they are going. And their assumptions and their beliefs, more often than not, are not in keeping with their greater purpose and true direction in life.

People may think God is great and inexplicable, but they try to use God as a kind of servant, an errand boy for their desires, their wishes and their difficulties. They say, "Well, what can God do for me? What will God's New Revelation do for me?"

You can see by this questioning that their attitude and approach are not appropriate. There is no reverence. There is no respect. There is no comprehension that they are dealing with something far greater than their understanding, that far exceeds their expectations, their values and their preferences. So what can God do for them but encourage them through life's changes and life's disappointments to come to this great engagement with a clearer intention and a more honest approach?

The New Message is here to save humanity from calamity and from subjugation in the universe as you begin to emerge into a Greater Community of life, a Greater Community in which you have always lived and with which you must now learn to contend.

It is also here to give individuals a new experience, a new foundation and the opportunity to restore their lives, to redeem themselves and to utilize their abilities and the power of Knowledge within themselves to be of service to a world whose needs and difficulties are escalating with each passing day.

Many people have given up on the search for greater meaning, or they never cultivated it to begin with. For them, the New Revelation will be a curiosity or an object of condemnation, something upon which they can project their fears, their judgments and their grievances without ever really understanding what they are looking at.

There will be all manner of response to this, of course, but it is important for those who are coming to this with an honest intention and with humility and sincerity to realize the power and the potency of God's Revelation and what it can mean for them—to restore them, to give them a greater purpose and direction, which already live within them.

You do not invent purpose and direction, for it is built in, you see. It is part of the blueprint of your deeper nature, beyond the realm of the intellect. Beyond debate and speculation this is. You can argue with it forever, but it just means that you do not understand.

It is important that people who come to the Revelation, sincerely, that they have an understanding, really, at the outset that they are dealing with something of a greater magnitude. It is not a mere teaching amongst other teachings. It is not simply a promising thing that will give them what they want in life. It is a whole other level altogether. That is why it is a New Message from God, the only Message from God in the world today.

This does not mean the New Message is going to craft a new life for you and give you a role to play, for that must come from within you—between you and yourself, between you and your engagement with life.

Many people will need the New Message to be the center of their practice and focus. And some people will be called to serve the New Message directly because that is their calling. But for many others, it will give them the strength to discern a greater direction and to give them a greater internal power and strength to make the necessary decisions and to turn the corners that must be turned to begin to move in a positive and meaningful direction.

There are many people in the world today who know they must prepare for something, who feel called to a greater participation, who have a sense that their life is more important than the mundane activities of the day. Some will not find their way in the religious traditions of the world because they are being prepared and called for something new in the world. They are more connected to the future than the past, and the future is calling them and pulling them forward.

There are people destined to receive God's Revelation and to study it and to apply it. They are not going to find their way anywhere else. If you are destined for something of this magnitude, you will not find satisfaction and fulfillment anywhere else. Try as you may, believe as hard as you can believe, try to alter your life like a tyrant, you still cannot make the primary engagement unless your life is pointed in the right direction and the nature of engagement that is meant for you can be clearly discerned and accepted.

It is for these people that the Revelation will provide a new life, not simply an enhancement of their old life, not simply a justification for what they have done or not done in the past. It is not simply a comfort to tell them, "Well, you are all right. What you have done is all right. It is okay."

No. The Revelation will make your errors more glaring, your disappointments more apparent, your lack of direction more deeply felt. It may even increase your suffering at the outset until you can discern the real gift of Revelation and to recognize that you are beginning a greater journey now, perhaps a journey you have been on for some time that is now taking a great step forward.

Here there is no room for compromise. You cannot make a deal with God. You cannot make a deal with your own purpose and destiny, for you cannot change these things. You can only avoid them, deny them or go through the process of accepting them and claiming them.

How your purpose will be expressed depends upon the changing circumstances of the world. So in this not all things are pre-determined, certainly not. Your success or failure is not only based upon your participation, but on the participation and readiness of others who are destined to play a significant role in your life. If they fail in this, it will affect the outcome for you, for your progress is dependent upon the development of certain other people.

This is not an individual pursuit where you try to enlighten yourself individually. It is a joining and a union with others for a greater purpose. If they fail, it will affect the outcome for you. If you fail, it will affect the outcome for them. That is why failure here has such great consequence.

You are still thinking as if you are living in Separation, so you cannot see that your destiny is tied with others. These are others who you will have to find in life. They will not be the charming personalities and the beautiful faces and the gracious social behavior that draw so many people. They will not even be people whom you could love or for whom you have some past association. Most of these people will not share your future even if you have had a distant past association with them. You will need Knowledge now, for it alone within you will know. It will see. It will respond.

If that other person is not ready, well, it will be a tragedy for you. That does not mean your life is over. It just means that another plan will have to be established for you. Your journey will be longer and more uncertain as a result.

There is so much to unlearn. There is so much conditioning that is not only counterproductive but actually destructive to the individual. There is so much driving expectation that leads you to commit yourself before you even know what you are doing in life, before you have made a connection with Knowledge, which alone holds for you your greater purpose and destiny.

THE GIFT OF A NEW LIFE

God would never reveal these things to the intellect, a part of your
mind that is conditioned by the world and is so unreliable and so
weak and so easily persuaded by other forces. No, the gift is given to
a deeper part of you that is not influenced by the world, that is not
influenced by your changing feelings and attitudes, your shifting
emotions, your hope, your fear, your ecstasy, your destitution—not
affected by any of this. It is living deep in the ocean [of your mind],
not on the turbulent surface.

Taking the Steps to Knowledge then becomes essential, or your life
will continue to be a vain pursuit—chasing people, chasing promises,
chasing ambition, chasing dreams, chasing hope, running away from
fear in all cases, terrified that you may be lost and alone, terrified that
your life will never come together.

Knowledge exists beyond the realm of desire and fear. That is why
it is sound. That is why it is strong. That is why it is unchanging,
and you cannot change it. This, however, represents your
redemption—that no matter what you think or do or have done or
have not done, the power of redemption lives within you.

God does not have to figure out your situation. The Lord of the
universe is not focused on your life. But God has put Knowledge
within you, and it holds your purpose and direction. It will find the
people you must find. It will bring correction, balance and harmony
to your life if you are able to discern it, to follow it and to apply it,
wherever that is necessary.

This is what creates a new life—not an old life with a few
enhancements; not an old life with a new belief system; not an old
life with a new set of clothes or a fancy religious explanation for
everything; not a tragic person dressed up for success; not a lonely,

isolated person who has now become socially acceptable because you say and do all the right things. You are not simply a billboard for someone else's beliefs. There is a greater promise for you.

God cares for you because God is providing you a new life. Otherwise, God would let everyone falter and fail and would not be concerned. This is what people actually believe because if you think God's Revelations were given centuries ago and God has nothing else to say to humanity, then you must conclude that God really does not care and has nothing more to say as humanity faces thresholds now, collectively, that it has never had to face before.

How will you deal with a declining world? How will you deal with intervention from predatory races from the universe, who are here to take advantage of human weakness and division? How will you deal with political and economic upheaval on a scale never seen before in the world? If you are honest with yourself, you will have to admit eventually that you do not even have a clue. Yet this is the condition of the world and what you will have to face, and everyone with you.

God is sending a preparation for the New World as part of the New Message. God is sending you the plans and the preparation to begin to establish a new life. There is the Message for the world and everyone in it. Then there is the Message for the individual who feels that they have a greater purpose and destiny in the world. You will have to decide if this speaks to you.

God did not invent your ideas and beliefs. God did not create your preferences and your fears. God did not create the world that is the product of everyone's preferences and fears. You cannot blame God for the social conditions of humanity. You cannot blame God for wars and cruelty, exploitation, slavery and poverty. That is all a human creation based upon greed and ignorance, based upon not enough people contributing enough to the world around them.

But God did create the presence of Knowledge within you, and only God's New Revelation makes this very clear, without an overlay of history and human interpretation to cloud your understanding. The stream is clear. The Message is pure. You are receiving it from its Source, instead of an interpretation that was made centuries later for human consumption.

To have a new life, you must do the work. It is not a spell that is put upon you. It is not taking some magic potion and having everything be different. It is not a form of addiction or intoxication.

You will have to do the work. You will have to take the risks. You will have to make the decisions. You will have to disappoint other people. You will have to disappoint your own goals and ambitions. You will have to change your plans.

This is where you become strong. This is where you become united within yourself. This is where you follow one voice instead of many voices in your mind. This is where your true allegiance emerges amongst your other commitments and obligations.

This is where you reclaim your strength and your self-confidence. This is where you stop behaving foolishly, giving your life away to silly and meaningless things. This is where you know who to choose to be with and how to resist the temptations that lead you elsewhere in life.

You become strong because Knowledge is within you. You endure difficulty because Knowledge is within you. You can face pain and loss, illness and even rejection from others you care about because the power of Knowledge is within you. And when you meet another who has developed this power, your relationship will be on a whole other level—extraordinary in the world, able to create far greater things than you alone could ever produce.

God gives you the source of your strength, but you must exercise its guidance, and you must develop the personal skills that allow you to become a vehicle for Knowledge—a person of power and integrity; a person who can inspire others and can bring confidence, comfort and direction to others.

This is God's New Revelation. This is what it is meant to produce. There must be many strong contributors in the world now, or humanity faces a great and precipitous decline.

Let this be your understanding.

CHAPTER 7

THE JOURNEY TO A NEW LIFE

As revealed to
Marshall Vian Summers
on December 21, 2012
in Boulder, Colorado

Life begins anew with the New Revelation. It is like a new lease on life. It is a new promise. It is a New Revelation from God, given now with the great Love of the Creator, given now with deep compassion for humanity's predicament, and difficulties, and troubled history, and destructive tendencies and so forth.

It is like having a new beginning for each person who can respond and for the world, which has now been touched once again by the hands and the Love of the Creator.

This sets a journey forth, which will be initiated by those who can respond to the New Revelation, who can receive its instruction and who can begin to learn what it has to teach and to naturally share this wisdom with others.

This is not merely meant to be a philosophy, which can be speculated upon and debated in the halls of academia or in the cafes and restaurants around the world. People who do that are not responding to the Revelation—not deeply, not honestly, not wholeheartedly.

The reconciliation with the Creator is a journey, you see—taking the Steps to Knowledge, beginning to bring one's life into order and clarity, resolving the dilemmas and the unforgiveness from the past, setting out on a new course with a great Revelation to guide one, to instruct one and to protect one.

It is like being given a gift of a new life for those who can receive and for those who will benefit from those who can receive. For the gift resonates from mind to mind and is demonstrated by those who are beginning to respond.

It is a great hope in a darkening world. It is a great promise for humanity that is losing its hope and its self-confidence.

The Messenger is in the world. He is here today. But he is an older man, and in his remaining years on Earth, he will proclaim the New Message to bring it to people so that they may hear and understand.

He will speak of the great promise for humanity. He will speak of the great challenges to humanity. He will speak of the power and the presence of Knowledge that lives within each person as God's great and most powerful endowment, waiting to be discovered. He will speak of taking the Steps to Knowledge. He will speak of bringing one's life in order and re-establishing one's integrity and inner certainty. He will speak of preparing for a new world—a world of environmental, economic and political instability. He will speak of following that which is powerful and has no fear, which is the great endowment.

He will speak of these things, you see, to give people confidence and to show the way. For this is not merely a promise, you see. This is not merely wishful thinking, for he has the preparation, for it is part of God's New Revelation. It speaks of God revealed, unveiled—the God of the Greater Community; the God of your life; the God of your heart; the God of your memory, deep memory; a God of your

Ancient Home; a God of your greater future; a God of your redemption; a God of your origin; a God that has sent you into the world for a greater purpose, which you have yet to discover, but which awaits you. Now you have the promise and the great opportunity to discover this and to take the steps, the great steps, to its realization and fulfillment.

With this, you are no longer lost in the world. It is like being a fish caught in the ocean. You are being reeled in by the Great Attraction of the Divine, and by the power of Knowledge within you, which responds to this alone, for this greater power has no other commitments except to its Source.

This is your promise of redemption. No matter how difficult or unhappy your life has become, no matter what you have done in the past, no matter how many regrets you may have, this is your redemption. For Knowledge within you is untainted by the world and untainted by your own misunderstanding and confusion. It remains pure within you.

This means that God is untainted by the history of the world and the history of religion. What is pure within you is untainted by all that has transpired—humanity's unhappy history and your unhappy history.

God is being experienced anew, like a new God—new to you, but timeless and unchanging.

So you begin the journey of many steps. You begin to learn how to direct your mind rather than being directed by it. You learn how to make real decisions with the certainty of Knowledge. You learn how to free yourself from certain situations and obligations that do not represent your destiny or your greater purpose here.

Long before this greater purpose is realized, you will be taking these steps to free yourself, to regain your lost life, to regain your power and your self-confidence.

For your greater purpose is not simply a big definition. It is a destiny. But to move in the direction of your destiny, you must be freed from the past sufficiently that you can move forward with a greater inspiration. So you begin the journey.

While everyone must learn certain things, each person's journey is unique to their situation, to their nature, to their history and to their circumstances. Each journey is unique in this way, but everyone is learning the same things and becoming liberated from the same things.

So you are not lost in Separation on the return to God. It is beginning now to reunite you with others in a profound and meaningful way. This is where your relationships of destiny will arise. This is where you will find true companionship, based not on familiarity or your personality, but upon a deeper resonance, for you can help each other in this journey, and you are taking this journey together. While it is mysterious and beyond the realm and the reach of the intellect, you support each other in doing that which has not been done before and having the courage and confidence to set out on a new adventure in life.

Here your greatest relationships will come into being. Here your greater strengths will be renewed. Here you will learn how to view the world with compassion and objectivity rather than with fear, longing and condemnation.

Here you will look on your past, no matter how troubled it may have been, to gain from it whatever wisdom it can provide. For it is teaching you what it means to live a life without Knowledge, a life without purpose, a life without true direction. It can serve you now if you can utilize it objectively. It is the demonstration that you must respond to the deeper calling of your life, that you must recognize the new God, which is the old God unveiled, and respond to what God has put within you to follow and to experience.

Here you set about resolving the dilemmas of your life so that you can regain your strength, which was lost before—lost to people and circumstances, lost to hopeless and meaningless endeavors, lost to unforgiveness and to condemnation of yourself and others.

Now you are beginning to reclaim this lost power, this lost part of your life. For you will need this strength for the future to face a new world of great change and uncertainty. You will need this strength to overcome your own fear and weaknesses, which have haunted you and disabled you before.

For now, you are on a journey. You only know this journey because you feel it, for something is stirring deep inside. This is the very beginning of your personal revelation, which will unfold incrementally as you proceed, and as long as you proceed, it will continue. As long as you keep taking steps, you will get up this mountain. You will find your way. You will loosen the bonds that held you down and kept you in the valleys below. You will see what decisions must be made and how to view the disappointments and the regrets from the past.

You will not understand this journey, for it is beyond the realm of your understanding. But you will feel it. You will sense it. And, at moments, you will recognize its utter necessity for your life. At other times, you will have to hold this feeling and to find others who can assist you in doing this. This is the natural return to that which is great within you.

Here God is not calling you out of the world, but to be in the world in an entirely new way—not as a weak, pathetic person; not as a mindless follower of your culture and your religion; not as someone who is corralled to work and to go to war, but as someone who was sent into the world for a greater purpose—as a contributor, as someone who can bring to others what they cannot give themselves and to bring resolution and strength in a unique way in the life of people around you.

The need is so very great and is growing every day. Human suffering and misery and deprivation are growing every day. And the risk of war between groups and nations over the remaining resources is growing every day. So the calling for redemption is powerful and must be sounded anew throughout the world, through a New Revelation from God.

You who are hearing this and reading this are amongst the first to respond. It is a calling that comes from the Source of your life, speaking to that part of you, that deeper part of you. It is this that will give you the power to respond, to go through periods of uncertainty, to resolve what seemed irresolvable before and to free you from what could not be freed before. For you are on the journey now, you see, a journey of many steps.

Knowledge knows the way. But your intellect will have to follow, for it is meant to serve the greater power within you, for it alone cannot be this power. God is calling you to respond. In your heart, you will respond.

Here you will learn about life in the universe. Here you will learn about the origin of the universe. Here you will learn about the miracle of Creation. Here you will gain a whole new understanding of humanity's evolution within a larger arena of life in the universe.

Here you will discover things that were never taught or revealed to humanity before, but only to certain sages and selected individuals. Here you will gain a greater education about the destiny of humanity and what will be required to free humanity in a universe where freedom is rare and where there is much competition for power.

Here you will learn things beyond your own personal interests. Here you will discover that you are living at a pivotal time in human history—a great turning point, a time of great challenge and difficulty, but also a time of great promise for a struggling humanity.

Here you will see beyond your fear and your previous obsessions. Here you will see beyond your former ideas. Here you will have a window into a greater life and a greater destiny, which can only be revealed to you through a Revelation from God.

This Revelation is now being given to all of humanity. It is not something that is simply imparted to one or two people. It is being given because the Messenger is in the world, and God has spoken again to give humanity a greater understanding of its reality, its greater promise and the challenges it must face and overcome.

This is the journey for all of humanity you see. But this is your journey as well. For you do not have a journey apart from this. Your part will be a small part, but a great and important part, a part that has the power to redeem you and to restore you, to give you dignity and purpose and a true sense of your wealth and greater abilities.

This is how God renews and restores you. It is not merely by believing in certain things or having certain ideas. It is by taking the journey, you see, and by engaging with the deeper Knowledge within you, which you will learn to do as you take the Steps to Knowledge.

Humanity has a greater journey to take to prepare for living in a new world of environmental instability, a world of declining resources and a growing population, a world where the risk of war and competition is greater than it has ever been before. But it is within this world that humanity can finally, out of necessity—great necessity—realize that it must cooperate to rescue human civilization and to secure its position in a universe that it must now contend with and comprehend.

It is not as if you were called out on a journey where everyone else is going somewhere different, for everyone is being called to this greater journey to play their small but essential parts.

But to do this, you must have the Power of Heaven within you to guide you. You must have the deeper strength of Knowledge within you to lead you forward, to carry you through periods of great uncertainty and confusion and to deal with the confusion, doubt and criticism of others. You need this greater strength more than you realize and all that it will bestow upon you, which you cannot produce for yourself.

Only God knows how to lead you to that which will redeem and restore you. You cannot figure it out. It is not an idea or a philosophy or a human invention. God gives you the pathway and calls you to return.

This is being given now with great clarity, for the Message is pure. It is uncontaminated by human history, human manipulation and the compromises of human adoption. It is pure. It is whole. It is complete. It is great in its scope. And yet it gives you the next step to take in your life.

For the Lord of all the universes speaks to your heart and to your soul, the most intimate place within you, where even the world cannot reach, that part of you the world cannot corrupt and overtake.

This is your freedom. This is your power. This is your destiny. This is what you set out to do before coming into this world. This is what you will reflect upon when you leave this world. Everything else will be forgotten. It will not be important then.

In a world of darkening skies and greater anxiety and confusion, you must have this certainty. But it must be a real certainty. It must have the Power of Heaven within it, and it must have your wholehearted support for it to fully reveal itself to you.

The journey will give you this opportunity to choose the Revelation again and again and again at each turning point, where you will stop in uncertainty as to what to do, afraid of what it might require. It is only by stepping forward, through that gate, over that threshold, that you will find that you are following that which is the most natural and the easiest thing to follow, and that any other decision you make

THE JOURNEY TO A NEW LIFE

is a decision to re-enter confusion and to fall back into the shadows of life.

There is part of you that is weak and part of you that is strong, part of you that is foolish and part of you that is wise. Certainly, that part of you that is weak must follow that part of you that is strong. That part of you that is foolish must follow that part of you that is wise. This is what it means to take the Steps to Knowledge, to return to that which is essential to your life and to take the journey, which is the most important journey in life you could ever take and will ever take.

Do not look to others for your cues, for you are being called by the Source now. Do not follow the crowd, for they are lost. But you are being called to be reclaimed and restored and renewed.

Look to your life. Listen within yourself. For you know you are not living the life you were meant to live. You are not fulfilling the purpose that you were really sent here to fulfill. This is a deeper honesty that has the power to overcome ambivalence and uncertainty, fear and the need for approval from others.

This is how God restores you, by liberating you from one thing after another so that your mind can be free and so that you can have the Power of Heaven within you to carry you forward.

For you must be a light in a world that is growing darker. You must have the strength and confidence to do this. You must have the strength to experience great joy and happiness in a world where joy and happiness seem to be disappearing, for that is part of your gift to others.

Here the Revelation is restoring you day by day, step by step, as you learn to bring strength and purpose to your affairs, as you learn about life in the universe around you and the meaning of human evolution. Here even your errors serve you. And the errors of others serve you to remind you of the great need for Knowledge and the need to receive and to reclaim your greater life.

This is the journey. This is the Power of Heaven. This is the promise for all of humanity. If enough people can take this journey and advance in this journey, the promise for humanity grows; the strength of humanity grows; the courage, purpose and integrity of humanity grows. This is the counterpoint to all that seems to be breaking down human civilization and the power and the potency and the creativity of humanity.

It is the journey—your journey, humanity's journey. This is the Power of Heaven working within you in the mundane circumstances of your life. This is the gift that gives, that restores, that renews, that liberates and that nourishes the deeper certainty in those around you.

CHAPTER 8

YOUR PURPOSE AND DESTINY

As revealed to
Marshall Vian Summers
on January 23, 2008
in Boulder, Colorado

There is a greater purpose for you in the world, a greater purpose that has brought you into the world, a greater purpose that is meant to serve the world that you see and the world to come. The reality of this purpose—its meaning and its expression—exists beyond the grasp of your intellect. It is something that resides deep within you. God has placed it deep within you, within a deeper Intelligence within you, an Intelligence that is called Knowledge.

Your attempt to understand this purpose with your intellect will always fall short of the mark, for the intellect was not designed to comprehend things of this magnitude. Trying to understand the deeper Mind of Knowledge is like trying to understand the Mind of God. It is better not to try.

What is important is to bring your life into a connection with this deeper Intelligence, into alliance with this deeper connection. This will give your mind, your intellect, all the work it could possibly assume.

People have lost their connection to God. Even people who claim to have religion have now created an understanding of God or have adopted it from their cultures, from their traditions that does not capture the real essence of the matter. It does not capture the mystery and the power and the potency of what your greater purpose really is. It represents the mind attempting to understand the reality of the Spirit. This attempt and this understanding will always be incomplete, will always be an approximation only.

It is important that you understand this, for you will try to understand, and perhaps you have already adopted many ideas. Perhaps you believe in things fervently regarding the reality of your deeper life, your connection to God and your greater purpose in the world. But the reality will always be beyond your grasp here.

But it is not beyond your experience, for it speaks through your experience. It is expressed through your experience. And in many cases, this kind of experience will be inexplicable, beyond comprehension, beyond definition.

Therefore, it is necessary to always allow part of your life to be mysterious and to treat this with reverence and with wonder, with expectation. You may feel you have a firm grasp on your affairs, your interactions with people, your work in the world, your duties, your activities, your obligations and so forth. But you must always remain wondrous of the mystery of your life. If you lose this sense of wonder, then you have lost your connection, your most vital connection, your lifeline to God and, temporarily at least, the possibility of experiencing and expressing a greater purpose in your life.

The world that you see will call this purpose out of you when you are ready. It is not just anything in the world. It will be something very specific. A situation, a set of circumstances, a very unique relationship, a great difficulty, a great and pressing need in the world will speak to you most profoundly, most directly. And every time you think of it, every time you re-experience it, it has the same deeper resonance with it.

It is as if you have found something with your name on it, something that speaks to you directly, something that stirs a greater sense of commitment within you. Again, you can imagine and believe you have a purpose, and perhaps this will change many times over. But it is not the same, you see.

Many people have given their ideas all the credibility and have forgotten the value and the meaning of their own experience. They just try to experience their ideas now. They want their experience to confirm their ideas, to validate their ideas, to demonstrate the truth and the efficacy of their ideas. But this is not it, you see.

It is people's fundamental insecurity that leads them to identify with their thoughts to this degree, that leads them to base their life on beliefs and assumptions, losing all the while the sense of mystery and uncertainty and expectation that comes with living close to life.

Here you must be without complete definition. Your life must be open. The possibilities must exist. Here you recognize that your ideas and beliefs are only helpful. They are not the absolute. They are only there to assist you in navigating the world. They are not there to define the world. They are only there to help you understand life, not to define life.

Here your sense of security must reach deeper, beyond the scope of your beliefs and assumptions and ideas to something much more sound and fundamental within you.

THE JOURNEY TO A NEW LIFE

You may believe fervently in God. You may believe fervently in the dictates of your religion, but this does not mean you have found this deeper foundation. This foundation is demonstrated and represented by Knowledge within you—the deeper Intelligence that the Creator of all life has placed there to guide you, to protect you and to lead you to a greater life and to a greater purpose in the world.

If you are circumscribed by your beliefs, how can God move you to do anything? As soon as your thinking or your activities begin to go beyond the boundaries you have set for yourself, you will feel frightened; you will feel anxious; you will feel uncertain. Your sense of identity will be shaken. You will be unsure of what you are doing. And you will likely withdraw, back into the safety, back into the confinement of your beliefs and assumptions.

It is pure arrogance to think that you understand God, that you understand what righteousness is, that you assume that you know God's Will and Purpose for you and for all of humanity. Yet many people make these assumptions and advocate these assumptions and condemn others for not agreeing with them.

If you are to have any hope of finding your greater purpose in the world and to move beyond the boundaries and the confinement of your own beliefs and assumptions, then you must open the door to life. You cannot live in a room of your own definitions. For this room becomes like a prison—a prison without windows where you cannot see out.

The door must be open. The windows must be open. The room gives your life definition and stability, but it must be open to life. Your understanding of God must evolve, must develop. To do so, you must be willing to go through periods of profound doubt and uncertainty as you go from one set of ideas or one level of understanding to another.

It is like the man on the trapeze. To go from one bar to another, he must let go. For a moment, he will not be holding on to anything, you see. But he has confidence that he can reach out and find the next bar, which will be waiting for him.

This is like your evolving understanding. To be a student, you cannot assume to be the master. To be a student, you must be willing to learn what you do not know already and to question your own assumptions.

But many people do not want to do this, for they think their beliefs are the truth. They think their beliefs are who they are and define their lives and give them certainty and stability in an uncertain world.

God has placed a greater purpose and a greater Intelligence within you. If you are to experience this, if you are to understand the messages that it sends to you, the signs that it gives you, and if you are to be able to follow the pathway it sets out for you, then you must be willing to go forward beyond the boundaries of your understanding, beyond the conventions of your culture or religion, beyond the expectations of others.

If you seek consensus for your views, you will always set your sights too low. You will always assume a lower set of standards for yourself. This is not your destiny, you see—to enter into the world and to become solidified in the world and the world's beliefs and expectations and so forth.

You are here to build a foundation for this greater purpose to be experienced, to be followed and to be expressed. This is your fundamental responsibility, and it will be your fundamental sense of fulfillment. For nothing else will fulfill the deeper need of your soul. Wealth, pleasure, indulgences, romance, accomplishment, recognition—none of these things will fulfill the deeper need of the soul, for this is the deeper need of your life.

Even if you are successful in garnering the wealth and the accolades of the world, your soul will remain hungry, its need unfulfilled, and you will be restless and anxious. Your successes and accomplishments will be very temporary and fleeting. Your restlessness will increase. Your sense of disappointment will grow. And you will see the shallowness of these successes. You will see that they do not fulfill you. They do not answer your deeper need, your deeper questions.

These can only be answered by the power and the presence that God has placed within you, a power and presence that you cannot control, that you cannot fully define, that you cannot use to gain what you want out of life.

In your heart, you know of what We speak of here. It is like a door you are afraid to open. It is like a stillness within you that you are afraid to experience. It is like the Presence that stands behind you that you are afraid to turn and to face—caught up in the world now with all of its conflicts and issues and campaigns, caught up in your work and your relationships with hardly a moment to reflect.

All of this waits for you. Whether you are conservative or progressive, whatever your political ideas and position, whatever your grievances and admonitions against others, this mystery, this calling, awaits you.

Perhaps you think at this moment, "Well, this is not the problem. I can face this. I know what this is. I can be with this." But when you begin to really respond, you will see how much resistance you have. You have been out of relationship with yourself for so long that now you are afraid of it. You resist it. It creates a sense of anxiety for you.

God, whether you believe in God or not, is still profoundly unsettling. As an experience rather than just an idea, God is profoundly unsettling—unsettling to your plans, to your goals, to your establishments, to your attachments.

There is shame there because you have done things you know are not right. You have regrets. You have things you do not want God to see, things you do not want to bring into this primary relationship. And so there is resistance.

You can attach yourself to the idea of God, but to the experience, well, that is another matter altogether. You may pray to God for what you want or to protect you or to protect those you love, but can you actually be with the relationship, the experience itself, without running away, without going and hiding somewhere?

People worship. They pray to God. They fall down on their knees. But they are afraid of the experience, the connection, the Presence, the Grace.

You come to God with your hands open. You come to God without assumptions, without admonitions, without declarations. In your prayers, in your meditations, whatever your spiritual practice, you bring yourself there as you are—with regrets, with anxiety, with uncertainty, with frustration—as you are, you bring yourself there.

You be with the silence. You learn to be with that silence. It is in this silence that Knowledge will speak to your mind, that God will communicate to you through the Intelligence that God has placed deep within you. It is here that you will learn to be patient and observant rather than nervous and demanding.

People want the answer to their lives: "Just tell me what my life is. Just show me what I have to do." But they are afraid of the relationship and the connection that will make this genuine and possible and effective in the future. Without the connection, you are still functioning at the level of ideas and assumptions.

You have to wait and receive, not receive all the things that you want necessarily, but to receive the presence and the connection—to let this slowly reshape your life, to re-orient your priorities, to set your values into some kind of coherence and unity within you.

For you cannot live a greater life based upon your life at this moment. You cannot jump from where you are to a different state of mind and awareness and participation in the world. There must be a profound shift within you, and this represents the inner work that must take place—inner work that is really mysterious, you see.

You may have a concept of it. You may value it. You may see it as necessary. But how it really takes place is beyond the grasp of the intellect entirely. It is the work of God within you.

You cannot simply adopt a program or an idea and say, "This is my higher purpose." For you are still the same old person with the same old ideas, expectations, habits and perceptions. These things will not allow you to assume a greater life. These things will keep you making the same mistakes over and over. These things will keep you right where you are.

You cannot simply adjust your wardrobe or do something cosmetic and claim that your life has changed, that you have changed, though people try to do this all the time. A new set of ideas, a new set of circumstances, perhaps new relationships, and they think their life is transformed. But nothing has really happened on the inside yet.

So at the outset, taking the Steps to Knowledge—beginning your journey to a higher purpose in life—is very mysterious. It does not look like anything is happening on the outside, necessarily, and you are impatient. You want results. You want to have your activities validated. You want to achieve your goals today, tomorrow.

But something is moving on the inside of you—imperceptible hour to hour, even day to day, but week to week and month to month, oh yes, something is really changing. And it is changing at a level that you cannot really understand. Do you have the patience and the perseverance to stay with this and to allow this change to happen?

You see, it is like cooking bread in the oven. Well, if you are taking it out every ten minutes to see if it is done, it will not cook. It will not go through its transformation. It will not become something edible and useful and beautiful.

That is like you. You need to let God create the change within you— the change of heart, the change of mind, the change of values and priorities, the willingness to change your circumstances, even your relationships. And you do this because you have a deep need, a great need—a need to know who you are and why you are here, what your life is for and what your life is about.

So most of the work at the outset is on the inside. It is to build a foundation within you, to create a shift within you. Otherwise, the assumption of higher purpose is just simply cosmetic. It is like wallpapering your room. It is creating a different appearance only.

To have a greater purpose in your life means you must have the foundation of Knowledge within you established, or you will run off into the world with your big ideas about who you are and why you are here. And God will not be able to help you. Only disappointment and disillusionment will bring you back to your senses, will bring you back to your humility, will bring you back to God.

As you begin to experience the evidence that there is a greater purpose for you, you will see that there have been signs all along the way—things holding you back, things discouraging you, things preventing you from having immediate gratification or immediate relationships with others, signs that indicated certain things about you that are relevant to your greater purpose: orientations in your life, unique and even peculiar kinds of interests.

You resonate with certain things profoundly, even illogically, for these are the signs. And they have been with you all along, all the way back into your childhood, you see, indicating something about you—a natural orientation, a natural interest or resonance that speaks to your future accomplishments and the possibility for living a greater life.

To begin to respond here, to move in a true direction and to allow your life to be reshaped and redirected by Knowledge within you gives you great joy and confirmation. At last, you begin to feel like you are one person instead of a group of divided and contentious factions—wanting different things, going in different directions, pulled by different forces.

You begin to feel like you have some kind of foundation within yourself, a center to your Being, that you are anchored somewhere genuine, instead of attached to circumstances, to people and to places alone. And this gives a great sense of strength and permanence.

For the sense of meaning of your life is purely an experience. Perhaps only later in hindsight will you really understand, but in the moment, it is an experience. And this allows you to settle down within yourself. This allows you to become still and observant within yourself. This teaches you the value of patience. It teaches you the meaning of waiting for things to come about, for the bread to cook in the oven, for things to take their course.

Over time, you will understand how change really takes place within people, how this greater shift occurs. What are its signs? What are the dangers that can prevent it from occurring? You will see these things because you will have experienced them yourself sufficiently that you can begin to gain a real understanding.

Here you must forego the idea of perfection and mastery, for those are obsessions. Those are ideas in the mind. If you are truly responding to the power and presence of Knowledge within you, then you will realize you must forego these things. You do not know what mastery is. You do not know what perfection is. These things must be shown to you over time.

The assumptions you have made based upon the values of your culture or your religion, well, God will take you beyond them to a greater understanding. But you must be willing to go. And when you go, you realize you really do not understand. What you thought you knew, what you thought was correct, now you are not sure.

Many people will not leave the shore here. They will not venture out in the open water. They want to stay firmly planted on the ground of their belief and understanding. To get on the boat that is floating, well, it is too scary for them. They will pitch their flag on the land. They will not venture out into the open water. And the world beyond their shores will remain unknown to them. And the journey that is for them, they will not undertake.

For when you leave that shore, you are without a firm foundation, it seems, for awhile. You are depending upon the raft that will take you to the further shore, and the further shore you cannot see. It is too far away.

You must leave the life that you have known for a new life. But to get there, you will be out on the open water, and Knowledge will be your raft. And those relationships that are strong with Knowledge, that remind you of Knowledge, will be your companionship and your assurance.

Though you may have great doubt and may want to return to the shore from which you have left, there will be something in you that will keep urging you onward: "Keep going. Do not stop. Keep heading out. Do not turn back."

And you will be afraid: "Oh, I left behind so many things. Maybe I've made a terrible mistake. And I've given up these things. Oh, my God, I should have them back. What am I doing?" But something within you says: "Keep going forward. Do not go back. You cannot go back."

God is trying to take you somewhere, you see, from inside you. There is no voice on high commanding you now. It is the certainty that God has placed within you—a certainty that you cannot change, that you cannot bargain with, that you cannot argue with, that you cannot alter according to your fears and preferences.

Some people think that their higher purpose is becoming fully engaged in what they really want. But this is rarely the case, you see, for what they think they want is really a substitute for something else, and they want God to validate their substitution. They want to use religion and spirituality to confirm that what they want is really what they should have and is the truth for them.

But, you see, you cannot change the direction that God has given you in life. You can only change your response to it. You will have to alter your expression of it given the circumstances of the world and adapt its expression to a certain extent, but you cannot change what it really is, you see. This is what gives you freedom—the freedom to finally be who and what you are, to follow the life that you were meant to live.

People think this is a loss of freedom when they cannot invent their life for themselves—be whatever they want, have whatever they want and do whatever they want, without any sense of responsibility. And though they may try a thousand things, they are still lost and frustrated and unfulfilled.

What your purpose is is something waiting to be discovered. The signs are there. You must allow it to change your life, even to put into question things you firmly believe you really want or must have for yourself. Even these things must be put in doubt, for there is something greater that is calling you—something greater than the satisfaction of your desires.

If you have the courage and integrity to respond to this, then you are beginning to have a real foundation in your life—something that cannot be seduced by the world, something that cannot be governed by the demands or expectations of others, something that will not be given away for convenience or for personal acquisition, something you do not bargain with, you see.

This is what gives you your strength, your power and your integrity. This is what inspires others. This is what makes the rendering of your true gifts possible, meaningful and effective.

Some people think they have already arrived: "This is my purpose. I am doing my purpose," when in fact they are only a quarter way up the mountain itself, perhaps moving in the right direction, but they have a long way to go. They think they have arrived, but really, they have only turned one of many corners. They must keep going. Knowledge will not let them become complacent or self-satisfied.

For there is much further to go, and your circumstances and the expression of what you are doing may change. So even if you think you have arrived, you have only really just begun.

This journey is what renews and rekindles your soul—the deeper joy and sense of confirmation about your life, the sense of belonging in life rather than simply being someone who's wandering around the world—aimless, directionless, like a rudderless ship out on the ocean, being blown by whatever wind and current exists at that moment, crashing on the shores, out of control.

Knowledge is your rudder. Knowledge is what keeps you moving in the right direction—weathering the storms of the world, weathering uncertainty, weathering self-doubt, weathering other people's disappointment in you.

So, you see, instead of talking about higher purpose in terms of the end result, We talk about the process of discovery and the journey you must follow because this is what matters.

You must be willing to go without knowing what the other shore is going to look like, how it is going to be for you. If you do not have this courage and this commitment, you will not get on the boat. You will not get on that ship to the New World. You will hesitate. You will fall back.

The ship is leaving. You will not get on it. You will stay in your little life with your little ideas. You will stay in your cell even though the door is open. You will close the doors and the windows because you do not want to look out. You will become like a person living in a little shell, encased in one's own ideas, identified with the past, identified with what you are accustomed to. And within you, your heart and soul will be starving and unfulfilled.

This is not what God intended for you, but it is a risk. It is the risk of being captivated by the world. It is the risk of becoming lost within yourself. It is the risk of being disconnected from the Source of your life and from the meaning and direction of your life. These risks are real and profound. Look around you, and you will see this to be the case.

Here you cannot look for consensus because if you are really responding, you may be the only person you know who is responding. Here your commitment to the truth must be greater than your obligation to others or your need for validation or approval from others.

God's calling will call you out, call you out of line with other people. And you shall take a path that others do not seem to be taking. And your fear of loneliness could be profound, but you will not be alone for long on this journey. You will have to take that risk. Here you are giving up bondage and submission to others for something great. But in the moment, it may not look like that at all, you see.

To be called is to be called out of line with others. Of course, they cannot follow. They are not being called at that moment. Even those who you think are spiritually educated may not be able to go with you, may not even understand what you are doing. Here you will begin to see the difference between ideology and inspiration, between self-definition and a greater purpose in life.

Great change is coming to the world. You have to be there for that. Great difficulty is coming for humanity. You have to be prepared to provide your service to the world. You cannot take forever to make up your mind or to drag yourself along, for you are trying to get somewhere, and the hour is late. To make your contribution to the world has to be done in time—at the right place with the right people.

If you are not in that place or with those people, then you are falling behind. For time here is of the essence. That is why there is always a sense of urgency around this. You are trying to get to a place of rendezvous with others who are meant to be with you, who are destined to be with you. You must get there yourself. If you are wandering around or falling down by the side of the road in doubt and confusion, you are not getting to your rendezvous.

You have an appointment with the world, you see. You were sent here for an appointment with the world. You must make that appointment. In your heart and soul, you will be trying to get to that appointment, and though you may misinterpret all the signs of this, it is there nonetheless.

As you can see, there are many dangers and risks. There are many pitfalls. There are many self-deceptions. There are many other forces in the world that will pull you away or hold you back. But the reality of your greater purpose is the most powerful voice there is.

But to know this, to experience this and to follow this, you must take this journey, you see, the journey of many steps. Taking the Steps to Knowledge—letting Knowledge reshape and reform your life; letting Knowledge take you into the future and build a new foundation; letting Knowledge take you to those circumstances, to those places, to those people that you need to connect with. For only Knowledge knows where the rendezvous will happen, when you must get there and how the journey can be undertaken.

Here you can only follow, but you must use your mind. You must use your talents. You must use your discernment and discretion. This will require you to gain as much strength as you can, to gather yourself together, to keep yourself together, to keep your focus intact, to keep your confidence intact, to keep moving in the right direction.

There is no passivity here. There is no hanging out here. It is living a committed life, and that commitment is what frees you—frees you from addiction; frees you from ambivalence; frees you from conflict;

frees you from self-harm; frees you from danger; frees you from giving your life away for beauty, for wealth, for charm. Frees you from all these things, you see. It frees you from these things, and it frees you for something greater. For there is freedom from and freedom for. But to gain the freedom for, you must gain the freedom from.

The power of Knowledge is calling you today. It is always calling you. No matter what you think about it, no matter what position you take regarding it, it is intact. It is powerful. It does not change. That is why it is the only reliable thing within you. It is the only thing trustworthy within you. It is the only thing that is certain within you.

Find that, then, that is certain, that is powerful, that has direction, that does not bargain or negotiate and follow that—taking the Steps each day, allowing your life to be re-arranged, allowing your values to change, allowing your mind to come into focus, allowing your true inclinations to take precedent over your distractions.

This is the great journey. This is what God wants for you. This is why God has placed Knowledge within you. This is what the world will need from you in the future. This is what your future relationships will be looking for in you: the evidence and the presence of Knowledge.

For you have an appointment with the world. You have a greater destiny in the world. And you have a greater purpose for being here. It is through this that you will know yourself and that you will know that God is in your life.

CHAPTER 9

BUILDING THE BRIDGE TO A NEW LIFE

As revealed to
Marshall Vian Summers
on February 25, 2008
in Boulder, Colorado

At a certain point, you will come to realize that this New Revelation is here to give you a new life. It is not simply to make improvements, or to sweeten it with a sense of spiritual meaning, or to condone your thoughts and beliefs or past actions with some kind of blessing from above.

At some point, you come to realize that the life you are living really is not appropriate for you. It is a compromise. And the compromise has been too great. It has been too thorough. It is a compromise with how you regard yourself, how you regard others and how you regard the world. And though this realization may be resisted, maybe it will be denied and further compromises will be sought, in actuality, it represents the beginning of a great hope for you.

For God knows that without Knowledge, the deeper Intelligence that has been placed within you, you would live a life of compromise. You would seek compromise for security, for approval, for wealth and advantage. You would seek compromise in order to avoid ridicule or criticism or condemnation or even social rejection. Compromise would permeate everything—your beliefs, your attitudes, your aspirations, your activities, your plans, your goals. This would increase to a point where you really had lost contact with who and what you are.

Now you have become a product of your society, a product of the expectations of society and a product of your own personal thinking. But you have lost contact with the deeper thread and meaning of your life. And even if you are successful and achieve your goals, it will be empty, and the joy will be short lived, and they will come at a great price of time, energy and effort. And the rewards will be momentary and fleeting.

This realization, which is so denied and avoided, is the beginning of a greater promise for you. Do not resist it. Do not argue against it. Do not complain that you may have to make great changes in your life. Of course you will because you are being given a new life—not a slightly better rendition of your old life, not simply new scenery or new faces or new forms of stimulation. This is not a cosmetic change. This is a change of a far greater importance and depth and meaning for you.

This is the kind of change your heart has been yearning for for so long, for such a long time have you been laboring. And now it seems to come to nothing. It seems you have failed the expectations of your culture. You might even feel you are a failure, that you have not fulfilled the goals and expectations of your family, your culture and even your religion. But in this seeming failure is a promise of a greater success. The old life must fail you, or you must fail it, in order to have this new opportunity, this opening in your life, this new beginning.

Many people simply want to have revelation as if it is some kind of appendage to their old life, [as if] spirituality is like a seasoning to the tastelessness of their life. It is something they are going to add on. Now they are going to be spiritual and do spiritual things and think spiritual thoughts and do activities that look edifying and uplifting.

But again, this is all for approval. This is all to try to seek more pleasure, more comfort and more security. The motivation for it is no different from the motivation that guides one to seek wealth and pleasure and escape from life. It is not authentic. As a result, it does not yield an authentic result. We are speaking of something very different here.

This new life, you do not know what it means yet. You do not know what it will look like yet because it is new. It is not your invention. It is not what you are accustomed to. And so you begin to turn this corner very slowly.

Even if there are major events in your life that have brought this awareness to you, the journey has many steps to allow you time to learn and to adapt and to gain a deeper foundation of confidence within yourself so that your life may become inner directed as opposed to being outer directed, that you may become a person of power, strength and integrity instead of someone who is mimicking the values of their culture.

Here many things will have to be learned anew. They will have to be re-evaluated. Many of your thoughts will have to be reconsidered. Many of your firmly held beliefs will have to be questioned, and in some cases even set aside. This is the price of freedom. This is the price one pays for having the opportunity to live a greater life, an authentic life, a life that is in keeping with Knowledge within [oneself], a life that fulfills the destiny that [one was] sent into the world to fulfill.

Until this turning point, you are only half alive. Yes, your heart is beating, and the blood is flowing through your veins, and your senses are reporting the world around you, and you are going through the motions of your life, meeting responsibilities and obligations and trying to seek some form of pleasure or reprieve. But it is an empty existence. The real meaning and value of your life has not yet been discovered.

Up until this point, Knowledge, the deeper Intelligence that God has placed within you to guide and protect you, will try to keep you from harm, will try to keep you and hold you back from making serious and long-lasting mistakes and commitments that will be in opposition to your ability to discover and to live a greater life in the future.

Here at this earlier stage Knowledge will seem latent within you, but really it is still trying to keep you out of trouble and to prevent you from giving your life away to another or to situations or to places, to people—to keep your life open.

Many people are in this earlier stage, of course. The emergence has not happened for them yet. When it will happen and how it will happen and even if it will happen is something that you cannot tell. It is a mystery.

You see, before this emergence, you really are just building a foundation to become a functional person in the world. You are building life skills. You are experiencing the pleasures and the pains of this world. You are seeking pleasure and avoiding pain and finding disappointment along the way.

This early preparation can be extremely important for what you will be able to realize, to accomplish and to communicate to others in the future. Even the most foolish mistakes you will make in this early phase can be very important in giving you wisdom—teaching you what is real, to value what is real, to help you discern what is good from what only looks good, to help you to discern your real inclinations from those impulses that represent your weakness and insecurity.

Perhaps in this earlier stage you will feel there is a Presence watching over you at times. You will sense that there is a Presence with you. And you will think from time to time that there probably is something greater for you to do in your life. But the realization has not really struck yet. It has not really rocked your foundation. It is only something you think about at the level of your intellect. It has not really penetrated your heart.

Your failures and your disillusionment here hold great promise for you. Your disappointment in yourself and in others and in the great pleasures for which you have paid such a great price—this paves the way for this realization. And this realization will not simply be a fleeting moment. It will be something that will change the course of your life. And you will not understand what has happened to you or the nature and purpose of the change until you have traveled afar in the second stage of your journey.

The guidelines for how to live that will be given here relate to this second stage of the journey of your life. They do not really refer to people who have not passed through this great threshold, who have not experienced this turning point. To them it will seem beneficial, but confusing. It will seem restraining. It will challenge their idea of freedom. It will seem to require too much effort and responsibility because they are not yet ready to make this effort or to assume this responsibility.

They are still trying to get out of life what they want. Beyond their basic needs, they are trying to get out of life what they want. They do not yet realize that they were sent into the world for a purpose. They have no memory of their Ancient Home, and so they think this life is all important, it is everything. They want to live for the moment, for themselves. So it is a very different awareness that one begins to gain after this great threshold. The guidelines for living here become not only helpful but essential for success.

The first requirement is to accept the great change that is happening and to leave the explanation open. You will not be able to understand it. Your intellect is referenced to your past and former life. It cannot account for what is occurring with you now and for the impulses that you feel now and for the orientation that is slowly emerging within you. Your intellect will try but will be unsuccessful at comprehending the meaning of this.

Some people try to go backwards here. They want to go back to whatever they thought gave them a sense of security and stability and self-assurance. But unfortunately they have gone too far now, for those attempts will be seen as empty, only pulling them back to a former life that they found to be unfulfilling—lacking in meaning, purpose and value. Now they are embarking on a new kind of journey, and they cannot define it.

Therefore, allow this change to occur. Do not try to define it. Do not even use ideas from other spiritual traditions to try to define it. Allow it to be a mystery, for to you it will be a mystery.

Mystery exists beyond the realm of the intellect. Honor this. Accept this. The Mystery is now beginning to emerge in your life, whereas before it was held back. Before, there was nowhere in your life for it to come forth—to guide you, to bless you and to prepare you. Now the Mystery is beginning to emerge. Let this happen.

You will become confused about what to do regarding your relationships with people primarily, and secondarily your relationship with where you live, the work that you do, your activities, your hobbies, your interests and so forth. Let this confusion exist. It is healthy. It is natural. It is part of the transition.

You are building a bridge to a new life. You are not yet fully living that new life. You are building a bridge. You are in transition. Transitions are confusing because you are moving from one understanding to another understanding, from one experience of life to another experience of life. The transitions mean that you cannot go back, and you have not gone far enough to go fully forward, so you have to be on this bridge, going through this transition.

Leave your future open. Set aside plans beyond what you must do to simply maintain yourself in the world. Here you must have trust that clarity will come, and clarity will come when you feel you are prepared to move forward and are willing to move forward into new territory.

As long as you hesitate, the clarity will not come. As long as you are bargaining and trying to work out some kind of deal to keep something from your old life, the certainty will not come. The clarity will not come because you have not yet turned that corner. It is like the answer is around the side of the mountain, and you have to go around that mountain to find it.

This is confusing for the intellect. But now the intellect must yield to a greater power within you, the power that God has put within you to guide you and to bless you and to prepare you for this greater life. You will still have to be very responsible in what you do and what you commit yourself to, in what you assign yourself to in life, in how you use your time and energy and so forth, but there is something greater moving in you now.

Next, do not go tell all your friends and family, for they will not understand. Unless one of them has turned this corner, they will think you are being foolish, or they will think that something bad has happened to you, or that you have been influenced by something that they are suspicious of. They might even think that you have gone mad.

Therefore, you must keep this new experience to yourself as much as possible. If you are fortunate, there will be one person, either within your family currently or someone you will meet who will give you a sign to move forward.

You will want to share your new experiences and the strangeness and the wonder of those thoughts and ideas that are coming to you, and of the change that you are feeling that is liberating you from the past. But you must be very careful who you share this with, for others will not understand. And their lack of understanding and their criticism and condemnation will really hurt you and rob you of confidence.

To move from being an outer-directed person to being an inner-directed person is a tremendous change, and you will feel very shaky at first. You will not feel very strong. You will be very uncertain of what you are doing. You will be like the little tender shoot in the great forest that must be protected until it gains enough strength to stand upon its own.

So there are dangers at this beginning, at this early part of your journey. Premature conclusions, indiscretion with others, self-doubt, the attempt to try to define your life—all these things are dangers because they can prevent you from proceeding onward. And once this journey begins, you must proceed onward. That is so important. Imagine that you are climbing a great mountain, well, once you begin to gain a little altitude, you do not want to have to go back. You need to go forward.

The Knowledge that God has placed within you will urge you to go onward, to keep your eyes open, your ears open, to be very watchful, to be very careful. Do not think that God is going to protect you now from every form of harm, and prevent injury and disappointment and tragedy for you. You must be very careful. This is part of gaining a greater awareness.

Previously, you were not careful. You were reckless. You were foolish, impulsive. Now you must become watchful, discerning, patient, careful. In doing this, you will see how you have been wasting your life, your time, your energy, over meaningless pursuits and over thinking that would never lead to resolution; and self-doubt, self-recrimination, judgment of others and the immensely superficial conversation that most people continue to maintain around you.

Next, you must gather your resources and conserve your energy so that you have time to be alone, to learn to be still and to listen. You will seek quiet now more than stimulation. You will find that the social activities around you will be aggravating and irritating to you, for you need something else now. You need to listen. You need to be quiet. You need to gain a greater connection to this emerging power within yourself.

This will change your priorities. This will change your desires. This will affect your decisions. And you will find that you will no longer be interested in doing things with other people that you did before. Things which were never really very fulfilling, now you will just want to avoid. You will see their emptiness, and you will not want them, and they will be an aggravation to you. And the pettiness and superficiality of people's conversations, and their habitual condemnation of others, you will find to be aggravating.

This is natural. This is what it means to come home to yourself, to find your real values, your real priorities, your natural inclinations as opposed to everything that has been conditioned into you. You will seek time away from other people. You will seek time alone. You will not want to have constant stimulation. You will need the confidence to do this. Most people cannot sit still for more than five seconds before they are driven out of themselves again. Here you must sit and listen. Gaze at nature. Listen to the sounds of the world, the natural world.

You will see here how your energy—your mental energy and your physical energy—have been misappropriated in the past, and you will want to conserve them, for you need them now. You are gathering your strength. You are gathering your resources. You are not throwing your life away. You want to plug up all the holes where your ship is leaking, where you are losing ground to others or to situations—through habit or through the designs of others.

The New Message will speak to you here, for it is imbued with the Power and the Mystery of God. And it is this Power and Mystery that are drawing you now. For what is really happening in your life is God is moving in you. God is moving you.

But this movement is a freedom from things at the outset. You have to disengage. You cannot take an old life into a new life, and so you are going through an incremental disengagement. Part of this disengagement is physical. It has to do with your activities and involvements with others. But much of it is internal. It is your ideas. It is your compulsions. It is what you think you should do, who you think you should be, what you should have or how you should be with others. For this is where the social conditioning really takes place.

And every day you move forward, you break these chains. They have less and less power over you. As you move up the mountain, the draw and the attraction of the lowlands are left behind, and you become freer and lighter and less burdened with the expectations of others and with your own needs that were never genuine to begin with.

During this time, limit your exposure to the media. Do not read a lot of books. Do not go to movies unless they are really inspirational, for you are gathering your strength. You are calling your strength to you. You are conserving your energy. You are paying attention to the inside now more than to the outside. You are moving away from the racket of the world. Allow this. Follow this. Strengthen this. For this is a natural inclination.

If there are longstanding friendships and they cannot follow you now, you will have to let them go, lovingly. They will fall away from you, for they cannot go this far up the mountain yet. You are going further than they can go yet. You have turned a corner they have not turned.

The most difficult thing in the early stages is people's obligation to others—to their friends, their family. The only exception to this obligation is the raising of your children, which you must do until they reach adulthood. But to all others, your relationship is now put into doubt. There are circumstances where you will have to care for an elderly or infirm parent, and that is appropriate. But beyond this, you are building your allegiance to God, and that will challenge your allegiance to others and their hold upon you. For many people, this is the most difficult challenge, the first great threshold in their preparation.

Do not explain yourself to others. Just say that there are deeper currents in your life and you are trying to follow them. There is deeper movement within your heart and you are trying to follow that. Tell them that you need time alone, time of quiet, time of retreat, time of re-evaluation. And do not feel you must respond to their persistent questions. You do not have to give them answers. Spare yourself the agony of trying to do this.

At some point, it will be necessary for you to begin to study the pathway that the New Message has provided: to take the Steps to Knowledge, to read the Wisdom from the Greater Community and to learn about Greater Community Spirituality. This will be like food to you, food for your heart, food for your soul.

You will need this now because this will give you strength and will confirm the greater movement of your life. It will give it greater clarity, greater definition, and will show you that this corner that you have turned represents your destiny and is not simply an accident in life. It is life itself, moving within you now. And the New Message will resonate with your deeper nature, a nature that is now slowly emerging within you. And this will bring new people into your life, people who also are turning a corner and have begun a greater journey.

It is important here that you not have firm beliefs. You do not need to accept firm beliefs. You are looking for a deeper experience now. The experience will be your foundation, not firm beliefs. You are escaping firm beliefs. You are venturing into a greater realm of revelation and natural experience. Everyone at the bottom of the mountain is entertaining firm beliefs, but firm beliefs do not enable you to get up this mountain and do not enable you to gain a higher elevation where you can see the truth of life around you as it will become evident.

Do not adopt firm beliefs. If you feel insecure, if you are unsure of yourself, it is fine; it is natural. Let the explanation be open. Do not attach yourself to a whole new set of beliefs. That is like going from one prison cell to another. Oh, it is a new place, but it is the same condition. Oh, it is new and exciting and reassuring, but it is the same old condition.

Allow the steps to reveal to you what the journey really is. It is not a journey that is understood by theorists or pundits or philosophers, idealists, academics or the general public. It is more of a mystical path, a deeper journey.

Its revelations will happen beyond the intellect, for it is not an intellectual journey. Your intellect will grow to accommodate it. And you will learn over time to gain a greater perspective and greater wisdom about many things. But an intellectual journey it is not.

For the intellect is a human invention. What created you and sent you into the world is not a human invention. What will reveal the greater life that you are destined to live and to fulfill is not a human invention. But it requires human participation, human wisdom, human ability, human trust and human discernment in order to manifest.

Here you do not give all your power away to God, thinking that God is going to guide you in everything. That is ridiculous. Here you give yourself greater authority within yourself that is not of your own making. But this authority requires that you become responsible, that you become honest, that you become self-determined. It will require you to follow things that are mysterious, but most of the time you will have to be doing very practical things.

If you are in a relationship and you have children, do not make any sudden moves in your life. Build the strength first. Build the connection to Knowledge within yourself. Learn to listen. Take retreat. Follow your natural inclinations. Share only part of the mystery with your husband or wife, for they may not be able to understand. Ask that they give you this time and this confidence, for things are emerging within your heart.

Maintain your duties and responsibilities, but take time to be with the presence of Knowledge within yourself. Take time to take the Steps to Knowledge, to study the Steps to Knowledge and to place yourself in a position where they can reveal their greater truth to you.

Tell your children that there is a greater power within them that will guide and protect them if they listen. Share with them your insights. But do not go too far in trying to share everything, for you are trying to build strength, and if you try to share everything, you are giving your strength away.

Do not try to take care of other people beyond your children or an elderly parent here, for you are gaining strength within yourself. You are learning to conserve your energy. You are fasting now, holding yourself back from giving yourself away everywhere, holding yourself in reserve.

Do not make any sudden decisions about your primary relationships if you are married with children, for in most cases it will be premature. A marriage here will be greatly challenged. Whether it can proceed will be determined by many things, which you may not be able to ascertain in the moment.

Your task is to follow the emergence of Knowledge within yourself, to be true to that, to be the recipient, to pull yourself in, to take the time it takes for a great emergence to happen within you. And do not be impatient, for it will emerge in its own time. You do not yet realize the magnitude of what is happening or how great its possibilities for the future will be.

Limit the influences around you. Be silent with those who proclaim themselves, who have great judgments upon the world. Do not enter into debate at this point. Do not contend with others. Do not argue the issues. Do not assert your ideas. That is not important now and will be counterproductive for you.

The power and the presence of Knowledge is emerging within you. That is the most important thing. You are learning to become strong and inner directed within yourself. That is the most important thing. Maintain your duties. Provide for your children. But hold this as the most important thing. For ultimately your greatest relationship is with God. Your greatest responsibility is to the Knowledge that God has placed within you to respond to, to follow and to express. This is an unparalleled freedom, but it requires great inner strength and forbearance.

These are guidelines for the beginning steps. Beyond this, you must learn to build the Four Pillars of your life—the Pillar of Relationships, the Pillar of Work, the Pillar of Health and the Pillar of Spiritual Development. You must learn of the Greater Community. You must learn about the mental environment. You must learn about relationships and higher purpose. This is all awaiting you. But first you must build the foundation, for without this foundation, you will not be able to penetrate the greater meaning, importance and application of these revelations that are contained within the New Message from God.

The foundation is so very important and requires great patience and forbearance. It is this patience and forbearance that will shift your allegiance away from your intellect and the admonitions of others to a greater power within you—the power of Knowledge, the power of God. You will never comprehend this power fully. You can never claim it for yourself. You will never be a master of it. You can never use it to try to be better than others. You cannot use it to get what you want. You cannot use it to gain wealth and power and pleasure. You can only learn to follow it and learn of the great journey up the mountain that was always prepared for you.

CHAPTER 10

COURAGE AND THE WILL TO PREPARE

As revealed to
Marshall Vian Summers
on April 9, 2011
in Boulder, Colorado

The mind is weak. Beliefs are easily challenged. Emotions are easily aroused. In the face of travail, one can lose heart and be easily discouraged. This is why people run from the truth, not because what they are facing is untrue, but because they do not have the strength to abide with it.

Their plans, their goals, their preferences, their involvements, their previous investments, everything can become so easily challenged in the face of the new world—a world of environmental change and social, political and economic upheaval; a more difficult world where humanity will have to face the damage that it has done to the world and its ability to support humanity. This is an immense challenge, and there are very few people, even amongst the experts, who can really face this.

People either go away from this entirely, or they hope that it is not true. They assure themselves that everything will work out fine or that humanity can deal with anything and everything. By that, they mean someone else can deal with it for them.

People cannot face reality because they are weak. They are governed by their thoughts, their feelings, their beliefs and the approval of others. So people follow each other around blindly, engage in long and meaningless conversations and indulge themselves in fantasies, hobbies and interests without ever reaching deeper within themselves or one another.

You can see what is real, for God gave you this ability. You can discern, in general terms, what is coming over the horizon because God has given you this ability. You can distinguish your deeper experience from your hopes, wishes and fears because God has given you this ability. It is these deeper abilities that are connected with the deeper Mind within you, the Mind We call Knowledge.

Knowledge is not afraid of the world. Knowledge is permanent; it is forever. It was with you before you came here, and it will be with you after you leave. It is not threatened by the world. But it is here on a mission. And for that mission to be fulfilled, it must prepare the rest of you—your mind and your body—for a greater service and participation in the world.

This requires that you face reality, both within yourself and around you out in the world. This, of course, requires a deeper honesty, beyond what you think of at this moment, an honest reckoning of your deeper experience and what Knowledge is really telling you that is happening in the world around you.

People look at difficult situations, and they hope for the best and assure themselves that it will be dealt with by someone, somehow, as if they were merely bystanders in life. But the man or woman of Knowledge looks and sees what is coming and sees if people have the courage and the will to prepare.

Here you face life clearly, objectively, with greater sobriety, but also with greater strength and compassion. As you learn to take the Steps to Knowledge, the deeper Mind within you, you begin to gain its sense of permanence and strength, certainty and determination. You see this lacking in others, and that is why they live such unfulfilling lives— chasing pleasures and dreams and fantasies, running away from anything that scares them or that challenges their ideas or notions.

But the calling is for you. The world is a proving ground for you. Regardless of what other people do or do not do, or say or do not say, the challenge is for you. You must understand this, or you will defray your responsibility onto others. "Well," you say, "what are people going to do? How can I share this with people? And how are people going to change?" That is trying to pass along the responsibility to someone else.

If you think of the general public, you will become discouraged most assuredly. But that is not where your focus needs to be. For you need to prepare for the Great Waves of change that are coming to the world. You need to prepare for humanity's emergence into a Greater Community of life in the universe. You need to prepare for the big events of your life, not just day-to-day affairs.

You need to prepare to build the Four Pillars of your life—the Pillar of your Relationships, the Pillar of your Work and Providership, the Pillar of your Health and the Pillar of your Spiritual Development. Like the four legs of a table, this is what upholds you and determines how great a life you can really live, and how much responsibility and wisdom you can really carry.

To begin to receive the New Revelation, you must have the courage and the will to prepare. This is not an ideology; this is not a belief system; this is not simply a host of ideas that you either like or dislike, agree with or disagree with. To think like this is to think foolishly and to not recognize the power and the meaning of the Revelation and what it calls for from you.

This has to do with honesty so much and what you tell yourself. Here people do not realize how much their lives are built upon dishonesty and the falsehoods they tell themselves. They are not honest with themselves, really, and therefore that is what they communicate to everyone and the world around them. And they think they are being honest because they are expressing what they think and feel. But they are really perpetrating falsehoods.

People build relationships upon falsehoods and false assumptions. It happens all the time. People build lives and careers and invest themselves heavily in things that never really had promise to begin with and that do not represent their greater calling for being here. It happens all the time, all around you: a great investment in romance, the great investment in business, the great investment that people make in things that really have very little to do with who they are and why they are here and what they are capable of really giving and comprehending.

The mind is weak. Your ideas and beliefs may be very firm, and you may defend them blindly, but it is still weak. It is a weakness to be fixed in your beliefs. It means you are not only foolish but arrogant on top of it.

You do not know who you are, you do not know why you are in the world, you do not know who sent you or what you are really here to do. All the pretense, all the admonitions, all the declarations that people make cannot conceal the fact that they are profoundly unaware of who they are, why they are here and what they are really doing.

People create very demanding lives and take on immense responsibilities before they have any notion of these greater things. And then they feel they must meet these responsibilities, which requires tremendous effort, of course, great suffering and struggle. But they never really have to think about the greater questions because they are too busy meeting their responsibilities.

But their responsibilities are not really authentic. They were built without a knowledge and understanding of their deeper nature, their deeper calling and their deeper responsibility to the Source of their lives.

That is why people are so grave, so unfulfilled, so conflicted, so confused. Oh, sure, they have great responsibilities, and they are being very responsible, and society admires that. But somehow they missed their calling in life, and now they are a slave to their responsibilities and expectations and the expectations of others.

And so all the wonder goes out of them. Spontaneity goes out of them. The creativity goes out of them. They are like hollow inside, walking through life, meeting their responsibilities, establishing a position in society perhaps, maybe even leading a nation. But they are hollow inside, empty, missing.

Knowledge for them is so distant, they would have to backtrack to find it. They would have to deeply explore beneath the surface of their mind to find it. But they are so committed on the outside that they dare not risk questioning their priorities and their responsibilities.

So they do not want to know. And they do not want to know anything that would challenge or threaten their plans, goals or activities. And so they are living blindly and are not utilizing the greater Intelligence that God has given them to guide them, to protect them and to prepare them for a greater life.

So they are disassociated from themselves. They are disassociated from God. They are disassociated from the truth. For them, the truth is all about perspective and ideas, which can easily be questioned and dismissed. They are too afraid to deal with the truth that cannot be dismissed, that has nothing to do with perspective. It only has to do with honesty.

You must realize your calling is a calling to prepare, for you are not ready for a greater life. You are not ready to understand and to follow Knowledge within yourself. You do not even know what it is yet. It is still a small and distant intermittent voice within you. You have not come into its proximity enough to understand its greater power and efficacy.

You see that it is a thousand times more powerful than your intellect. [Yet] you will think it is a tool of the intellect, a tool to help you get what you want and to avoid difficulty.

This misunderstanding is there for almost everyone at the outset. They think God is their servant. God is going to give them what they want. God is going to help them with all their problems. God is going to enable them to fulfill their dreams and goals, thinking [this] comes from God.

It takes so very long to unlearn these things and to have the honesty and the courage to question them, to walk around them and look at them objectively, to see if they are really true, if there is any truth there at all, and to break free of the social conditioning that makes you a slave to other people's approval and expectations.

That is why God's first purpose is to unburden you, for you are burdened with the unnecessary. You are struggling with things that can never be and have little promise. You are a slave to your culture, to your family, to your religion, to ideas and beliefs that are not founded upon Knowledge. And that which is founded upon Knowledge, you cannot easily discern.

It is like the needle in the haystack, as people say. Well, you have to remove a lot of hay to find that needle. That is what your preparation is largely about—to remove that which is false, that which is unreal, that which you are bound to that you desire, that you do not really need. It is not necessary, and therefore it is a distraction and an obsession for you.

People fall in love with other people based upon images and personality and seductions—people that could never take the greater journey with them, not in a million years. And yet, oh, they are so devoted they give their life away. They are obsessed—personality obsession. They are obsessed, and they call that love. As if love were some kind of drug you become addicted to, and then you have to go through withdrawal, which is immensely difficult. There is substance addiction and personality addiction. It is not love. It is obsession.

Knowledge will guide you to the people, the individuals, who really have promise for your life, who really have the possibility of becoming significant and meaningful relationships for you. We say "possibility" because they too have to prepare, for no one is really ready for the greater realities of life. That is like asking children to be ready to go out and work in the world like their parents. They are not ready for that.

In like manner, you are not ready to live a life of a greater purpose. And so the preparation becomes the emphasis; your honesty becomes the emphasis; your patience and your determination become the emphasis.

For, you see, only Knowledge brings you to Knowledge. All your other reasons—wealth, pleasure, peace, love, romance—all these things have to be set aside as you go along. You cannot take them up the mountain with you. They are far too heavy and unnecessary.

So the student is in a process of undoing things they have already set in motion and breaking free of false expectations, goals, plans and desires. They do not become ascetic here; they simply become honest—basic, simple, deep honesty. It is not a lifestyle. You are not giving up all pleasures; you are not withdrawing from the world; you are not living a life of extreme abstinence. You are just becoming honest, to the point where you are no longer lying to yourself and to other people, and to the point where you can see your tendency to do this and can correct it and objectify it within your own experience.

To prepare requires courage. You must face things you have not faced before. You must consider things you have not considered before. You must question your beliefs and your assumptions, and the beliefs and assumptions of your culture, your family and even your religion, if necessary.

You find this courage because it is coming from a deeper place within you—beneath the surface of the mind; beneath the turbulent, confused and chaotic surface of your mind into a deeper place where there is certainty, wisdom and Knowledge.

People are so frightened and so driven and so compulsive, they cannot be still for five seconds. They close their eyes to begin meditation, and their mind is like a wild animal—going everywhere, like all the channels of your television running at once, going from here and there and everywhere.

You must step back from this and not identify with this. It is just the mind, trying to process all of its impressions, information and problem solving—either reasonably and logically or in fantastic ways, as if you are in a dream.

The courage comes from recognizing and feeling a deeper need within yourself. It is really responding to Knowledge, perhaps very faintly and intermittently at first, but Knowledge is calling you to respond.

This is how God speaks to you, you see. The clouds do not part and a great voice speaks, thundering through the mountains, calling your name. No, even for the saints and the great Messengers, the process is the same. Everything else is just storytelling, to induce belief and submission.

You feel the deeper need to respond. You feel the need to understand where you need to go in life. You do not want your life to end up like all the people you are seeing around you. You do not want to become a slave to your mind or to your culture. You do not want to have empty relationships. You do not want to work, slavishly, to build wealth.

So you have to really look at your life. What is available to you? What limits you, on the outside? And then, even more importantly, what limits you on the inside? Which is nothing more than your beliefs, assumptions, desires and fears—all those things that are vaporous and have little substance in reality.

The moon still rises, the sun still shines, the seasons pass, the grasses grow, the birds fly, the fishes swim—so what difference do your thoughts make, except to either cloud or clarify your perception?

It is not a question of creating your own reality, for people use that to build, they think, a better fantasy to replace the miserable one they are living in now. But fantasies are miserable if you attempt to live them because they are not in accordance with reality or Knowledge within yourself. And the more you invest, the more hazardous your life becomes and the more you are afraid of the world. You are afraid of change; you are afraid of loss; you are afraid of honesty.

God asks you to be honest. From this, you can begin to discern a greater pathway for yourself, a greater calling in your life, a greater association beyond the visible realm and a new foundation for participating with others in ways that are marvelous and productive.

The will to prepare and courage...Courage is taking on difficult things without any kind of certain outcome. It is not following the easy path, where everything is laid out for you: You go and work in your father's business, so you never have to think about what you are really here to do. You have children before you are ready so that they will determine the responsibilities of your life. You get married before you have any clue of what you are doing and the direction you need to go. Therefore, your marriage determines your life and ends up looking like everyone else.

The world is the way it is based upon how many people are responding to their greater calling and purpose of their life. If the percentage is tiny, well, the world is always in a state of travail and conflict, at the edge of conflict, at the edge of breakdown.

People become slavish, like herds of animals—driven into war, driven into needless consumption, driven into political persuasions, driven into religious beliefs when they have no real sense of who they are or what they are doing.

People live at the surface of the mind, which is like the surface of the ocean—turbulent, swept by the winds of the world, one day calm, the next day stirred up, even violent. If you were to look at the surface from the side of a ship, the ocean would make no sense. You could not discern its greater movements. You could not discern that beneath the surface, waters are moving like a conveyor belt all over the world.

You would not understand the life that lives within that ocean. You would not understand how organized, though complex, the system of the oceans and the climate and the Earth really are. You would just see turbulence and try to adapt to that, like those sailing a ship. They have learned to understand currents and patterns of wind over time, so they have a greater understanding because they had the need and the courage to prepare for that.

The winds of the world are sweeping your mind around—drawing you in, upsetting you, overwhelming you, delighting you, intriguing you, terrifying you. How can you ever find yourself here? How can you ever discern the greater direction of your life here?

You must withdraw from these things, to a great degree, to have any possibility of coming into proximity to Knowledge within yourself. So you will feel the natural inclination to withdraw from social activities, from the media, from many things, for a period of time so that you can have the opportunity to discern your deeper experience.

The Lord of the universes has provided the Steps to Knowledge, a powerful preparation that you could not provide for yourself. You follow this, and as you do so, that which is true becomes stronger, and that which is false becomes weaker. As you follow this, you become more circumspect about your life and your decisions, more careful with your time and your involvements with others, more discerning of the world around you.

As the mind becomes more quiet, you begin to perceive things you did not see before. You hear things you did not hear before. You begin to respond increasingly to Knowledge within yourself and to Knowledge within others. And you see how you can tell the difference between Knowledge and everything else.

The Angelic Presence watches to see who can respond to the calling and then see if they have the will to prepare and the courage to take the Steps to Knowledge, to climb this mountain, a mountain that they cannot discern and do not understand; [to see] who can take a real journey in life, a substantial and powerful journey. The Angelic Presence watches to see who can respond to Knowledge and who can prepare.

The preparation then becomes the proving ground. It does not matter if you have a great destiny to do something very significant in the world if you cannot prepare for that. And the preparation requires more unlearning than learning—breaking free, going through periods of profound confusion and uncertainty as you release your old ideas and approach a greater understanding.

Like the man on the trapeze—he must let go of one bar to reach the next. And so those intervals can be very empty for people. You are not who you used to be, but you have not yet become what you are meant to become, so you go through periods of emptiness and uncertainty. But that is natural and part of learning. That is an integral part of preparation.

What carries you through this is Knowledge, and your faith in Knowledge, and the evidence of Knowledge that you are beginning to live and have acquired thus far, and the evidence of Knowledge in the lives of people who inspire you.

You must go through this preparation. You are not yet where you need to be within yourself or even within your position in life yet to really comprehend and then respond to a greater calling.

So the calling is to prepare, and to prepare you must have deeper courage. And that deeper courage comes from your honesty. You are developing a deeper honesty. And the motivation for all of these things comes from Knowledge.

Knowledge will bring you to Knowledge. Knowledge will carry you through periods of uncertainty. Knowledge is permanent. Your experience of it may vary as your proximity to it varies, but it is constant. It is not confused. It is the master; you are the student.

But here you also need other teachers, students who are more advanced than you in learning and applying the New Revelation. You will need, if you can, to learn of the Messenger himself, who is in the world now. It is a great blessing that he is here and that you can learn from him. For when he is gone, then the Messenger will be gone.

People will have to then rely upon their comprehension, which is a very dangerous thing when people are not really well prepared. Mistakes can be made easily, and the Message can be altered, confused and diluted. Others can come to assume positions of power and leadership who were never really authorized to do this by the Greater Powers.

To live at the time of Revelation, to live at the time of the Messenger, is immensely important. You will not have a personal relationship with him—he does not have time to have personal relationships with hundreds and thousands of people—but you can learn from him. Be grateful that you are living at a time when he is here with you. He is an older man; he is not going to be here forever.

You need powerful influences on the outside and on the inside to navigate the confusion, the complexity and even the deceptions that exist within you, and certainly to navigate a changing and increasingly unstable world.

You need the power of Knowledge. You also need strong companions. And you need powerful examples from others to inspire you and to help you see if you are making a mistake in your comprehension or application.

Some people come to the New Revelation and just want to be blessed by it, and think that from now on the blessing will just take care of everything for them. They want to be on spiritual welfare, thinking God is just going to provide and provide and provide, and they just have to be accepting of the miracles they think will be coming to them. But, you see, this is dishonest.

To be in a genuine relationship requires real participation. It requires preparation. It requires effort. It requires an investment of time and energy. It involves change and adaptation.

You cannot just marry someone and think that they are just going to do what you think they should do, and you are not going to do anything for them; you are not going to have to change to be with them. People actually get married with this attitude. It is amazing. It is so profoundly ignorant, but it is sadly true.

The calling is to respond. Then the calling is to prepare. And the preparation is significant. But even during the preparation, you will have the opportunity to contribute to others. That contribution will come out of whatever advancement you can make in your preparation. Even your demonstration of responding to Knowledge is a powerful teaching to others. Even your unwillingness to make certain compromises with yourself and others is a powerful demonstration.

Here you teach, automatically, as you learn, if your learning is authentic. In fact, you teach anyway because you are always demonstrating what you value and what you believe in. So as you value something far greater and more significant, then that becomes part of your demonstration to others.

Here your relationships change. Old relationships can fall away, for they cannot take the journey with you, and new relations appear on the horizon.

This is part of the miracle of your life, the miracle of Knowledge—the miracle of God's Plan of redemption and restoration going on behind the scenes, going on beyond the realm of human activity, speculation, deception and belief.

You have come to the world to assume a greater responsibility, a greater purpose, to give something specific to certain people in certain situations. You have no idea what this is, and so you must prepare. Knowledge must prepare you, and Knowledge must reveal where you must go and what you must do to achieve these things.

You have to govern your own mind and keep it supporting you. You have to exert authority over your thoughts and your behaviors. But you cannot determine the greater purpose of your life. For that you must follow a greater power, and the greater power is within Knowledge within you and within the Revelation itself.

It is within all the world's great religions if it can be discerned. But the world's great religions have become so overlaid with conventions and beliefs and assumptions and associations that you would need a very skillful teacher to pass through all of this, to reach the essence of what these religions really mean and are indicating. They are all pathways to Knowledge, you see. But this is not really evident from the surface.

This is part of the reason that the New Revelation is here and that We have come again, now, to speak to you as well as to the Messenger. We speak to you through the Revelation, and Our message for you is very great. And the time and the requirement is very great. And the change upon the world is very great.

It is time to become strong and courageous, honest, compassionate and determined. Then you are really being alive and not like a walking dead person. Then you are really creative. Then your mind is connected to Knowledge, and the Separation within you is beginning to end. Then your life becomes a demonstration of God's Presence and Power in the world, not only by great things you might do, but by your simple activities and just by the way you are, what you do and what you do not do.

God saves you from the inside out. God reclaims the separated through Knowledge. Nations and worlds become stronger, more stable, more creative based upon how much Knowledge is being expressed and demonstrated within their own populations.

This is true here and throughout the universe. It is all beyond human comprehension and the realm and the reach of the intellect. But your intellect plays its part. It is a critical tool of communication and navigation in the world. But it must have a greater guide and power, or it tries to become God itself, with tragic consequences.

You have been called. Now you must prepare. The preparation is within you, and it is being provided by the Lord of the universe. Now you must find the courage to take the Steps to Knowledge, and with this courage, the patience, and the perseverance, and the discretion and the discernment as over time you learn to discern what is true from what is false, what is really good from what only looks good.

This is the journey. It is the most natural and essential journey in life. And you are blessed to learn of it and its gifts to you.

CHAPTER 11

BUILDING STRENGTH AND RESILIENCE

As revealed to
Marshall Vian Summers
on April 5, 2010
in Boulder, Colorado

When you reach that point in your life when you begin to seriously think that you might have a greater purpose in being here—a recognition that is certainly waiting for you and has been waiting for you for a very long time—when you begin to think of this, you must consider the issue of strength.

People assume they are ready for things they are not ready for. They assume, if given the opportunity, if given the encouragement, that they could undertake a more important set of tasks in their life. But the truth is they do not have the strength, and they do not yet have the capacity, and so great opportunities may come to them, but they will not be able to see it or to receive it. It will seem too demanding, too inconvenient, too disruptive to their current activities, too complex, too confusing, or just too difficult.

But what is a great opportunity but an opportunity to do something of a greater magnitude in your life? And this will certainly require more of you than your current activities require. It will require greater strength, greater courage, greater self-confidence, greater self-honesty. It will require many things from you.

Therefore, you prepare for your greater purpose before you know what it is. You prepare in part by building the qualities that you will need to have, the skills and abilities you will need to undertake a greater activity in life. Otherwise, you will not be able to rise to the occasion when that wonderful moment of recognition occurs, where you realize that a greater opportunity has come to you.

Many people do not realize that they have missed great turning points in their lives thus far, particularly if they are older, simply because they could not respond. They could not meet a challenge. They could not change their current trajectory. They could not break free of commitments and obligations. They did not have the strength. So strength is very important.

If We were to tell you, you had to be able to climb this mountain over here, and it was a very high mountain and required skill, We would not just send you over there to begin hiking up the sides. It would begin a whole process of preparation. You do not know what it is like to scale a mountain like this. You do not know what it requires. You do not have the wisdom to understand its dangers and the opportunities you will have along the way. These things must all be learned ahead of time before you take on something really big.

Your greater purpose is like climbing a mountain, and in the same way, you must prepare for the climb itself. You must prepare by building strength and resilience and consistency. Not only must you be able to mount the effort, you must be able to sustain that effort, over time. And in the case of considering your greater purpose in life, it is a great deal of time. It is the rest of your life.

So the strength building begins now, and in some ways, you have been doing this all along—building consistency, building hopefully self-honesty, building courage to take risks, building courage to communicate with people and to resolve difficulties and dilemmas, building the skill to maintain responsibilities and to learn how to become a responsible person. This is all foundation building for what may come later, and what will come later if you prepare for this consciously.

Here your hopes and dreams must be based upon a solid foundation. You must be building the capacity for greater truth and the strength and the resilience to carry greater truth in the world and to follow what the truth will indicate for you—even if it is difficult, even if it is undesirable. [For] even the most wonderful opportunity will have undesirable aspects and will require tremendous effort to be sustained over time, to be accomplished and fulfilled. No matter what your current circumstances, you have the opportunity to build strength and to build resilience, to maintain and to sustain your responsibilities and to increase your responsibilities.

This, of course, is moving in an opposite direction that many people are moving today. They want to escape responsibilities. They want to avoid responsibilities. But what is having a greater purpose in life but assuming a far greater set of responsibilities? Now you have to live a greater life [with] greater actions, greater courage, greater strength and greater self-honesty.

Here you break away from other people who are trying to have as much benefit with as little investment as possible, and you set off on a different pathway. You will not be totally alone in this, but you will have to leave many people behind, for they have not come to the point of recognition that they must prepare for something greater in their lives.

You could say, with some accuracy, that everything you have been doing in life thus far is a preparation for your greater purpose—building character, acquiring skills, recognizing the importance of self-honesty, learning how to communicate effectively with other people and to work with other people, offsetting your own dangerous or unwarranted tendencies. All of these things can be established through the course of life itself.

When you reach that point of realizing that you do have a greater purpose and that you have to prepare for it, you will be able to look back on your life and see how certain essential skills were necessary for you to reach this vantage point. And you will appreciate the long periods of time where you had to maintain and to sustain your activities, even if they did not represent your greatest aspirations. You will appreciate the simple contributions of people along the way, even people who demanded great things of you and set a high standard for you. Even people who were difficult to deal with—even they helped you build a foundation.

This recognition will give you a very different understanding of your past and a greater appreciation for everyone who has participated in your life, for everyone has either shown you what you must do or has shown you what you must not do. Through their recommendations and demonstration, they are showing you all things you need to know to finally become honest with yourself and to realize you are here for a greater purpose.

In preparing for your greater purpose, you will be carrying out study activities, learning The Way of Knowledge, building the Four Pillars of your life, and this will go on for quite awhile. You will become impatient, thinking, "Well, where is the exciting part of this? Where is the glory? Where is the inspiration? Where is the great achievement? I am just living this mundane life and carrying out all of these activities."

You will have moments like this certainly because you are not used to building a real foundation. You wanted to give the minimum effort for the maximum reward. And now you are finding out the effort required is far greater than what you have done before, and more mysterious because you cannot define the outcome. In fact, you may not even be sure what will happen next.

The Angelic Presence needs to know that you have the courage and the stamina to do what will be required. Before they reveal to you anything really important, they want to see if you can sustain the effort, if you can be responsible enough, if you can correct your damaging self-tendencies, if you can be consistent, and if you can be strong.

This is so very important because it is a great tragedy when something significant is given to a person or a group of people and they cannot sustain it, and it fails. It is a failure for them individually. It is a failure in their relationships. And it is a failure to those who have given them this greater opportunity in life.

People who give themselves glorious goals, glorious missions, glorious definitions, they are just talking to themselves. They do not know what they are doing. They are living in fantasy, and if they are given something real, they will create a fantasy out of that. They will make it bigger than it really is at the moment. They will embellish it with their desires and their ambitions. They will color it with their perceptions and their beliefs. They will turn it into something else until it is unrecognizable. That is why the ambitious are never given things of importance to do until they can demonstrate a greater allegiance, a greater allegiance to Knowledge.

The strength that We speak of is not the kind of strength to simply mount a great effort for a short period of time, to go run ten miles or to finish a project on time, or to mount a great effort in the moment, even in service to another. The strength that We speak of is the strength to take a long journey, to go through long periods where you are not sure what you are doing, to be able to face your own self-doubt and the doubt you have in the wisdom of your actions. It is the strength to carry a greater responsibility in life over a long period of time.

Certainly, at this moment not many people have such a strength because they have never developed it in the other activities of their lives. They have never had to take care of other people. They have never perhaps had to provide for other people, especially if they are wealthy and affluent. They have never had to sustain their work over a longer period of time to achieve an important goal. They gave up when the going got difficult. They capitulated to their friends' persuasions. They could not go the distance. It is not because they lacked inherent talent. It is not because they were evil or wrong. It is simply because they had never developed the skill and the capacity to do greater things.

So when someone is called by God to something greater than simply manage one's affairs with a reasonable degree of success, there is a period of trial and error. There is a long period of preparation before the real purpose of your efforts is revealed to you.

Even for the Messenger himself, he had to demonstrate his ability to carry forward for many years without really knowing the outcome, without understanding clearly what his efforts were leading to and the great responsibility that he would have to accept and maintain.

But people are impatient. They want the answers now. They want to hear the outcome, and then they will decide if they will take the journey. But in life you must take the journey to find the outcome. If it is a true journey—and not simply a romance, not simply a fantasy of some kind—this is the truth of the situation. You must have that strength, that courage, that faith, for here faith really means something.

A greater purpose is not your creation. You do not invent it based upon your desires and your own discernment. It does not happen on your terms. It does not reveal itself according to your wishes or demands. That is what makes it greater.

So, you see, you are going to have to prepare not only to carry this greater purpose, you are going to have to prepare even to discern that you have a greater purpose. You do this first by building the Four Pillars of your life—the Pillar of Relationships, the Pillar of Work, the Pillar of Health and the Pillar of Spiritual Development. All of these Pillars must be strong enough to sustain a greater calling in life. If they are not yet that strong, then that calling cannot be given to you without causing serious damage to you and without creating the possibility of failure for those who are watching over your life.

So, you see, it is a very, very careful thing. It is not for the idle. It is not for the ambitious. It is not for the curiosity seeker. You must have the most serious intent. And you must be committed for the long term, you see. So it is to develop these abilities and these qualities that really represents the work at the outset.

So many people claim they are ready, they are strong, oh, they have done all these things in their life, but when confronted with something of this magnitude, they fall away soon. They do not have the self-confidence. They do not have the trust in the Greater Powers. They are driven by ambition, and when it appears that their greater purpose is not there to serve their ambition, they fade away quickly.

You must build the Four Pillars of your life, beginning right now. And then you learn The Way of Knowledge and take the Steps to Knowledge, which you can do right now. And then you begin a deep evaluation of your life and circumstances, particularly your relationships with people, with places and with the activities of your life to see what is really true and should be sustained and what does not have this strength and this certainty and this purpose.

This, of course, requires objectivity and considerable courage. Even developing the ability to be objective is a great challenge for many people. So there are prerequisites here. The prerequisites include the things We have mentioned: self-honesty, responsibility, consistency, duty, discernment, mental and physical health, real work abilities and skills and honesty in your relationships—all very important things just to live a good life in the world, but essential to carry on a greater purpose, and to be able to sustain that purpose, and to fulfill it correctly as it was meant to be fulfilled.

Here you are working towards something greater, and you are leaving the definition of that open so that you may experience it as you proceed.

Most people, if they were told the real outcome of their purpose, they would feel tremendously inadequate because they are not prepared. And perhaps they would run the other way, thinking, "Well, this isn't what I want to do with my life!" They would think that because they do not know their real wishes. They are not honest enough with themselves to know the yearning of their own heart. They are still chasing dreams they have invested in so greatly: romance, wealth, beauty, charm, excitement. They are chasing all these things, committing themselves to things that have no value, no permanence and no real reward at the end.

Do not worry about them. They are not your problem, unless you happen to be aligned with one of them or married to one of them. Then you do have a problem. But your challenge is before you. You cannot have a bargain here. You cannot bargain with the truth. And you cannot bargain with God or the Angelic Presence. They hold the pathway for you. You can either take it or not. You can either begin to prepare for it or you cannot. The decision is yours. There are no deals to be made. The truth is not compromised at this level, you see.

You go because you know you must go because Knowledge, the deeper Intelligence within you, is confirming that you must proceed. And it is this Knowledge, instead of your will power, or the strength and conviction of your beliefs, that will really be the foundation that will sustain you through difficult and uncertain times ahead.

The world is facing the Great Waves of change—great environmental change, great economic upheaval, great conflict and deprivation. All these things can destroy your focus and cast you away. You are building strength not only for your greater purpose, but to be able to weather and sustain yourself through the difficult times ahead. God is giving you this wisdom to save your life, not only in terms of your greater achievement in the world, but to sustain your life, period. You do not realize the gravity of what is to come to the world. Even if you are worried about events, you still do not see the power of these times.

It is Knowledge that will carry you forward, for it has unlimited strength and capacity, far exceeding what you can achieve through will power alone or through the strength and conviction of your ideas. They are fragile in the face of great change in the world, and they will not carry you through the long preparation that is before you, and they will not give you the real courage that you need to proceed when others around you are falling away or falling into despair.

That is why you take the Steps to Knowledge as part of your preparation, for you need to discover the source of your strength and inspiration. You need to find the wisdom that God has put within you that will enable you to navigate the difficult times ahead and to sustain yourself through your own difficulties and through the difficulties of life around you.

You must be very resilient, very strong and very compassionate if you are going to take a greater journey in life. Beyond mere survival, this is the promise of fulfillment for you, for nothing else in the world will fulfill you. None of the rewards that people pander [to] or that people worship or give themselves to completely will fulfill the deeper need of the soul. Here you must have a different focus in life. Your desires and your roles cannot simply be conditioned by your society or by your family and their values, for there is a greater calling for you. And that is why We are giving you this teaching as part of your preparation.

When you come to know this is the truth about your life, you will have turned an important corner, and you will set out on a different stage of your journey in the world—a different stage with new realizations and new requirements as well.

Though this may be a time of uncertainty for you, it is a time of great promise. It is a time of great excitement for those who watch over you and your life. For your success is not only for you, but it is for them. And it is for the many people who will benefit from your gifts and who will be inspired by your actions to undertake a greater purpose and journey for themselves.

Let this be your understanding.

CHAPTER 12

PREPARING FOR A GREATER ROLE IN THE WORLD

As revealed to
Marshall Vian Summers
on May 6, 2011
in Boulder, Colorado

Every person has been sent into the world for a greater purpose, a purpose greater than their own designs, goals and ambitions. This purpose is connected to the purpose of others, and to the condition of their cultures and societies, and ultimately to the whole world.

If this purpose can be clearly realized over time, then you will see that it is in harmony with everyone else's higher purpose. And though your ultimate role may be very specific, only dealing with certain people and certain situations, this role resonates with the higher purpose of everyone here.

But discovering this higher purpose is not an intellectual pursuit. It is not a puzzle that you put together. It is not an ideology that you frame and reinforce. If anything, it is a falling away of beliefs and assumptions, a falling away of false goals and aimless ambitions. For your purpose is there already, waiting to be discovered, but it is overshadowed and overlaid with so many other things.

That is why this is not an intellectual pursuit. This is why you must come to the Great Practices of God's New Revelation. They were designed to bring you to this greater realization and, in the process, bring your life into balance and harmony, to cease the endless conflicts and grievances that haunt you, confuse you and keep you in a diffused state.

Your gifts are for others, which means you cannot bring them out of yourself. It is through true engagement with others that your greater gifts begin to emerge. They do not come all at once because the discovery does not come all at once. It is not like you have a great realization and from then on everything is clear. For this is not the case at all.

Your purpose will ultimately reveal a role for you, a role in conjunction with others, a role in conjunction with certain needs in the world that you are designed to attend to and to address. This is not a role that you make up for yourself, based upon whatever spiritual ideas you have put together for yourself.

People do this, of course. They want to become an enlightened teacher, an avatar, a spiritual prince or princess, a prophet. But you cannot create these roles. They are really given to you from Greater Powers, and you must work very hard to assume them and to function within them successfully and beneficially.

People want to use all their normal attitudes and beliefs to attain a higher goal and a higher role in life. But it is all of these approaches and assumptions and habits of thinking that must be penetrated if you are to make your true discovery and to be ready to assume the role, and the greater responsibility that goes along with it.

That is why you must follow a preparation not of your own making. That is why you must not build your understanding based upon a patchwork of different ideas that you have picked from this tradition and that tradition, an eclectic approach, because it is all based on preference and assumption. You must follow a path that has the power to change these things, for it is these things that are keeping you where you are, that are deceiving you and holding you back.

Only God knows your true role. Only those who are sent to oversee your development know why you are truly here. In this, you must have great faith and have the humility and self-confidence to prepare for something you do not yet understand and perhaps cannot even picture or imagine for yourself.

You do not know your deeper nature. You do not yet comprehend your true design. You do not yet realize your greater potential and abilities, which must be cultivated gradually, carefully and productively over time.

While you are going through the daily motions of your life, and dealing with problems that arise, and fear and anxiety that are always with you, there is a greater process underway that is trying to move forward despite your difficulties and your misunderstandings.

This is not a process that you learn about in your universities. This is not a process you read about in a book and think you understand it. Yes, there are insights that are helpful in supporting you in undertaking this greater preparation. Yes, there is great wisdom that is shared in words. But the journey and preparation are essentially mysterious because they are functioning beyond the realm and the reach of the intellect.

Ultimately, it is your role, as you begin to discern it from afar, that will tell you what you must be, do and have in this world to assume this mantle of greater responsibility.

You plot your course according to the role that is finally coming into view after many turns of the road, after many undulations of the pathway. After many false assumptions, and false attempts and false conclusions, you begin to discern there is a role for you. This usually arises when you are around the people who are meant to be a part of this and who can point you in the right direction. Alone and isolated, you will not see it, not clearly enough for it to be a point on the compass where you can plot your course.

Then there is always the danger that your role will change because the circumstances have changed, and the other people who were to be involved have fallen by the wayside and cannot make the sacred rendezvous. So while your goal is predetermined, its expression is not, and the circumstances under which it can arise can change dramatically in the face of other events.

This is not a solo pursuit. This is not perfecting your Separation. This is not enlightening yourself. That is delusional. This is preparing for a greater participation in life in conjunction with certain other individuals. Pray they do not fail the rendezvous with you.

This is a Plan born of the Creator. It is the Plan to unite those who must be united and to separate those who must be separated, to engage those who must be engaged and to create a process where greater wisdom and clarity can be realized.

But human beings make different decisions. They respond from their own conditioning and disposition. They can miss the signs. They can misinterpret the engagement. They can go off course at any moment and stay off course for the rest of their lives. The degree of error is significant. So We are talking about probabilities and possibilities.

PREPARING FOR A GREATER ROLE
IN THE WORLD

People can fail. People can destroy their own motivation. People can wreck their physical or mental health. People can give their lives away to other things, which is very common, and therefore not be prepared for the engagement and, as a result, miss it altogether.

That is why your studenthood in the New Revelation is so very important. To follow this, you must build over time great trust and self-confidence, and confidence in the power of Knowledge—the deeper Intelligence within you to guide you and to hold you back when that is necessary.

People want many things. People believe in many things. People have preconceived notions. People have fixed beliefs. People have made great investments in their lives, which must be challenged and reconsidered.

Within each person is the desire for union and also the desire for Separation because you have two minds within you. You have your worldly mind, which is completely invested in trying to be healthy and successful as an individual—a rather fruitless pursuit. And then there is the deeper Mind of Knowledge within you, which holds for you your greater purpose and is completely committed to your discovering and expressing this.

That is why learning to follow Knowledge is so important. Here the choices are fundamental, but can be difficult to discern at the outset because you are so used to following your worldly mind and the minds of others, to be a slave to your beliefs and assumptions, your desires and your fears. It is to liberate you from these things that represents the great redemption that God's New Revelation is providing.

But you still must do the work. You still must take the journey. You still must engage yourself in the deep evaluation of your life to discern what is real from what is not, what is necessary from what is not, what can go forward with you and what cannot.

That is why in presenting the Revelation, We must always caution against the common mistakes and assumptions that people will make. The way is certain, but it is very particular. It is weaving a thread through the deep jungle, and you must be able to discern the pathway and know how to deal with obstacles that arise within you and around you. The path is specific for you. That is why you cannot follow generally believed assumptions and conceptions because as you proceed, these will not be helpful to you.

To assume a greater role in life is a transformation that is mysterious and yet phenomenal. It represents a level of success that is unmatched by anything else. In fact, any other kind of success pales in comparison. This is where your great humanitarians, your great creators, your great scientists, your great artists, your great leaders, your great contributors emerge, more often than not from very humble beginnings.

Do not disqualify yourself, therefore. You do not know enough about yourself to do this. Do not think that you understand, for you do not yet understand. Do not presume you will assume a great and recognizable role, for this is very unlikely. Do not think that you are too foolish or stupid or weak to undertake this journey, for you do not know the source of your own strength.

The path will open before you if you can keep your mind clear, which is a very great challenge and represents part of the training and development that you must undergo to assume a greater life and a greater purpose.

Do not worry about your friend or these other people. You cannot determine their destiny, their greater destiny. Do not try to take someone with you because they may not be ready, and their pathway may diverge from yours. Here you can love people intensely, but you cannot hold onto them tightly if you are to be a source of freedom and truth in your life.

In hearing Our words, you can begin to see some of the challenges for you and how different this is from the way you currently think and behave, and how much strength and determination you must bring to that which calls to you.

Some people think roles are false, like you have a role in a play, or a role in a movie or are just playacting a role. But that is not what We speak of here. We are talking about your destiny in the world. We are talking about what you agreed to do before you came into the world. We are talking about something that only Knowledge within you really understands. It will guide you, but you must learn to recognize it and follow it, without really knowing the journey or what the end result will look like.

For even if you could see your role clearly from a distance, by the time you finally get there, it will be different. It will have changed. Circumstances will have changed. For there are many factors and forces that come into play here. It is not just you and what you bring to your journey. It is the condition of the world. It is the success or failure of others who are destined to participate with you. It is all the things that could happen along the way.

The world is hazardous. Though beautiful and enchanting, it is hazardous. It has physical hazards. It has psychological hazards. Therefore, over time, you become very careful and discerning. You reserve your speech. You do not follow crowds. You hold yourself back so that you may see and know. You take refuge from the world for periods of time, trying to gain your own direction and to sustain it and support it.

Your friends change, your associations change, your priorities change, your values change—naturally, as they must, as you become ever more honest with yourself, and as your life becomes more authentic and inner directed.

The beginning student always thinks they are on the verge of great discovery. The intermediate student thinks that the next step is going to be really the big step. The advancing student just realizes that they need to take the next step.

It is very hard for the beginning student to understand this great change in attitude and approach, but this is part of the preparation, an essential part of the preparation. It is a transformation from being governed by your thoughts and the thoughts of your culture, religion and society to being directed by the power and presence of Knowledge.

Here you still have thoughts and feelings, desires and fears, but they are all brought into alignment through the power of Knowledge. And you can see them clearly because you realize that who you are is not your mind. That is a great discovery that will be yours as you proceed, as you climb this greater mountain and are able to see the landscape of the world—a landscape you could not see before—and the relation of all things, which you could not see before when you were in the valleys and the forests below.

The journey requires great precautions and many reminders. And since not all of you can be with the Messenger, and he cannot be with you at all times, We give this wisdom to you to consider, both as a revelation and as a constant and ongoing reminder.

The journey is being directed by Greater Powers. This is what reunites you with your Source and with those who sent you into the world. It does not unite you with all people, but with certain people for a greater purpose.

Here your thoughts will change. Your beliefs will change. Your assumptions will change. Your perception will become more refined and more far reaching. Your intuition will grow. You will gain greater discretion, for you realize that everything you say is important, and you do not want to commit yourself incorrectly to people or situations that cannot support you in taking this greater journey that represents the true calling of your life.

Other people will frustrate you, confuse you, disappoint you. You will want them to go with you, but they may not be able to. You will want them to understand you, but they do not understand. You do not want to take the journey alone, but you must get up this mountain on your own accord and through your own effort.

You will gain new relationships on this mountain, relationships of a much higher caliber, of a much greater integrity, with a greater promise. But you cannot wait at the bottom for others to go with you. You must set out and take the Steps to Knowledge.

It will be disheartening at first to realize how few people that you thought you knew really do not know you and cannot take this journey with you. They cannot even appreciate it. They think of you as their brother, or their sister, or their friend, or their son or their daughter. They cannot see that you are a greater individual with a greater destiny.

You will try to share the Revelation with others, and you will find blank faces or people who say they understand, but they really cannot receive it yet. It will be shocking. You may be feeling very alone. But that does not mean that the calling is not real and that you do not have a greater destiny.

Let this destiny be undefined. It will not be grandiose. Only in the rarest occasions will people garner attention from the world around them, for this brings grave misfortune.

The Greater Powers are here to prepare you and to protect you so that that which is true and real within you may emerge and become strong in the world. But at the beginning, it is a delicate little shoot in the ground, unable to withstand the harsh forces of the world. That is why it must be cultivated and cared for and protected. You cannot have other people trampling upon it with their ignorance and their foolishness and their lack of sincerity. Keep the jewel within your heart. Do not throw it out onto the street.

You do not yet know what you are here to give. You are in preparation. You are practicing. Your life is moving. Your life is changing. What a great blessing this is. For in your former life, there was no hope for your fulfillment and success. Whether you attain wealth or not, whether you attain love or not, your soul remains unfulfilled. And over time, a great emptiness will descend.

PREPARING FOR A GREATER ROLE
IN THE WORLD

You are being rescued from a deadly mundanity. You are being saved for a greater purpose. Your true connection with the Source of your life and with greater individuals in the world is being prepared, but you have a long way to go. It is a journey of many steps, and you must take them all.

As you become more advanced, your role will come into view, only periodically. This is important because here you will have an understanding of the difference between that role and where you are today, and certainly the difference between that role and where you were when you first began. And you will use this to plot your course and to gauge your progress, for you can see that role requires a greater strength and many other skills that you have not yet fully developed.

Here self-honesty becomes a great checking point for yourself—not just honesty of how you feel, or that you can tell others your problems, but a deeper honesty at the level of Knowledge. For you can feel Knowledge within yourself, deep beneath the surface of the mind. It will tell you if you must stop or change course. And if it is silent, you must keep going. You may bring to Knowledge your plans, your desires and your preferences. If it is silent, that means that these things are not important. You will gain this greater awareness as you proceed, and it will become your barometer. It will become your compass.

Knowledge does not chat away like your personal mind. It is a steady force, a great attraction, a power pulling you, pulling you along. It is amazingly intelligent because it is connected to the Creator. It is this that will get you up the mountain, for it is determined and relentless. It is this that will be the source of your strength, not your personal will or the strength of your affirmations. It is this that will keep you from giving your life away to people, to places or to things that do not represent your destiny.

Yet it is still. It is quiet. But it is powerful. It will not answer all your questions, most of which are simply an expression of your fear and anxiety. It will not explain everything to you, for the signs of your life come without explanation. The Way you follow, it does not explain anything.

As you proceed, your mind will become lighter. You will take joy in simple things. You will feel love for many people. You will become compassionate for everyone you see, regardless of their errors or their dilemmas. Your mind will not be critical and condemning. It will be compassionate, and yet it will be focused.

It is a very different state from the state you are in today, which is very chaotic and very much driven by perception and emotions. But this greater state has a stability to it that the world cannot destroy, a strength that the world cannot undermine.

It will bring to you relationships of a caliber that you could never find otherwise. It will bring you to a life for which you are completely designed. And you will finally discover that what you know and what you want truly are the same.

CHAPTER 13

THE GREAT TRUTH

As revealed to
Marshall Vian Summers
on December 25, 2007
in Boulder, Colorado

There is a great truth about your being in the world, a great truth that you cannot alter, that you cannot change, that you cannot remake into something that you would prefer or something that other people would expect of you. The great truth is about you and your relationship with the world and why you have been sent into the world at this particular time, under these particular circumstances. For it is no accident that you are here and that you have come at this time.

Though it seems to be a mystery to you, it is very clear to those who have sent you. And while your memory of your Ancient Home is erased—or seemingly so, as you enter this life, as you take the long journey to becoming a human being, to becoming part of a society, part of a family, a part of civilization—that memory still resides within you. And though perhaps you cannot see it now or feel its presence, it holds true nonetheless.

For there is a great truth that you have been sent into the world, to serve the world in a unique way in concert with certain other individuals, within certain circumstances. You are designed and equipped to do this, and that is why you have a unique nature and personality. That is why you have certain inherent strengths and predispositions.

Yet without this greater purpose to guide you and to give meaning and value to your life, how can you understand your individual nature? How can you understand yourself? You cannot, for you are meant to be part of something greater, something beyond your own evaluation, something beyond the identity that your family or culture alone can give you.

People try to endlessly remake themselves, recreate themselves, create better versions of themselves or try to be like someone else entirely. And they expend their life force doing this—their time, their energy, their resources—trying to be something without knowing what they really are.

They undertake this fruitless endeavor because they have not found their greater purpose. They do not understand themselves within a larger context. They do not see that they were perfectly designed for something that they have not yet discovered.

You can try to be like someone else. You can try to alter yourself. You can try to remake yourself. You can hide behind your clothing. You can hide behind your style or fashion. But you cannot change what God has created and why God has created you in the way that you are.

Certainly you will have to mitigate any destructive behavior or patterns of thought. Certainly you will have to manage yourself properly. This is required of everyone.

But the great truth remains that you are especially designed for something that you have not yet discovered. And it is wise that you not think that you have discovered this yet. Even if you are moving in the right direction, even if you have responded to some of the clues and the signs, do not assume that you have found your role yet, for that can only be recognized more in hindsight than in foresight.

Do not think you have arrived, for you are still climbing the lower slopes of this great mountain, and you know not what lies ahead, or what will be required of you, or how your life will be reshaped and refocused by the many changes that will come your way and that indeed are coming to the world as a whole.

The great truth also reveals that what God created in you is not reflected in your thinking, in the patterns of your thinking, in your habitual thinking, or even in your highest beliefs or ideals. For who you are is not your mind—the mind that absorbs you every moment of the day, the mind that captivates you, the mind that you live in, at the surface of this mind. That is what the world has taught you to think. That is what you believe you have to do and to be and to have to be acceptable within the social environment of your family and society perhaps, or whatever group you identify with.

But there is a deeper Mind within you, for the great truth reveals that you are born with two minds—a mind to think with, a mind to deal with all the particulars of your life, and then a deeper Mind, the Mind called Knowledge, the Mind that God created. It is meant to guide you, and to protect you, and to take you to fulfilling your greater purpose for coming here; to show you the way; to lead you to the steps and the thresholds, the engagements and the relationships that will be part of this greater service to humanity.

This, then, is a great revelation for you if you can understand it—that you are sent into the world for a greater purpose and that who you are is not the mind that preoccupies you.

Your mind may try to believe in everything that seems to be righteous and holy and appropriate. You may imagine yourself to be a saint or an avatar or a righteous person. Whatever the mind tries to create and idolize and worship and denounce and advocate is still only happening at the surface. Deeper down, far below the surface, there is a greater Mind, the Mind of Knowledge, the Mind that God has created.

Now indeed God has created your capacity to think, which is a marvelous creation. But the world, in all of its confusion and error, in all of its desperation and anxiety, has filled your mind, has conditioned your mind, has conditioned your thinking and, as a result, your behavior and your attitudes and your perception.

The greater Mind within you, Knowledge, can—if you will learn to follow it and to recognize it—also shape your thinking, your attitudes, your beliefs and your perceptions. But it is a very different influence overall.

This is a great problem for people who feel that they are spiritual, that they are undergoing spiritual development, spiritual renewal, spiritual education. They are still trying to follow the world and follow something deeper that is more mysterious within themselves. Perhaps they call this the Will of God. Perhaps they call this the word of their great teacher or their saint. Perhaps they call this the Holy Spirit.

Whatever they call it, it is beyond the definitions of the mind because Knowledge, deep within you, is the Mind that God created. And the mind that the world has created, well, it cannot grasp this. It cannot understand this. It can only yield to it and follow.

For Knowledge is mysterious. It does not function according to the dictates of the world or to any kind of invention or rationality. Ultimately, it will make perfect sense and will reveal itself to be a perfect guide, but in the long process of rebuilding your relationship with Knowledge, it will seem mysterious and inexplicable. You will doubt it, and often. There are times you will not want it. It will seem a great nuisance and problem for you. And at other times, you will recognize it is the most precious part of yourself, the most precious gift of the Creator, your most valuable asset.

All true spiritual development is rebuilding your relationship with Knowledge and allowing it to become the center of your life and the true guide of your life. You see, no matter what your religious affiliation, no matter what your spiritual practice, the truth of Knowledge is within you. And this is a greater truth because it is a truth from God.

You cannot change this truth. You cannot rework it or make it fit in with what you want or what you think you must do, have or be. The more you try to tamper with it, the more it seems to escape and become inaccessible to you.

Knowledge within you knows why you are here. It knows whom you must meet in this life. It knows where you are trying to go to and where you must go to. It does not waver. It is not indecisive. It is like a great magnetism pulling you in a certain direction.

And from where you stand at any given moment, you will not understand. "What is this attraction? What is this pull? Why do I feel I must do this? Why must I leave here and go there? Why can't I commit myself to this situation? Why must I venture alone when I can be with these people? Why must I say no to this opportunity and yes to this opportunity?"

There are no good explanations, really, though you will try, yes, and it is understandable. The poor mind will do whatever it can to try to understand what this greater power is once it has been recognized. But ultimately your intellect must yield to the power of Spirit that God has created for you and within you.

For God knows why you are here, what you are here to do, who you are here to meet and the difficulties of being in the world. That is why God has given you a perfect guiding Intelligence—something beyond the intellect entirely; something beyond definition; something beyond the limits and boundaries of religion, culture, philosophy; something that cannot be corrupted or applied for personal gain and wealth.

For you cannot use Knowledge to get what you want. You can only follow Knowledge with the understanding that it will take you to where you need to be and that it will shield you from those things that could captivate and dominate your life.

When you really recognize this, when you have reached a high enough place on the mountain to see the value of this, you will recognize it is the greatest gift that God could give you.

For if God gave you what you wanted alone, your addictions would become deeper; your confusion would increase; you would become attached to things that do not reflect your greater purpose and nature; you would commit yourself to things with no value, no future; you would give yourself over to the demands and expectations of others; you would capitulate to the insanity of the world and all of its desperate pursuits and conflicts.

A loving Creator would not do this to you. Just like a loving parent would not give the infant child anything that child wants to play with—sharp objects or dangerous weapons or dangerous situations.

You are like a child in the world, you see. You want things that are not good for you. You are afraid of things that could really help you. You think you perhaps understand who you are and what you are doing, but there is great uncertainty beneath all this. You are driven by the expectations of others. You are commanded by your culture or the dictates of your religion. You are indeed a slave to other forces, you see, and this is inevitable if Knowledge within you cannot be experienced and rediscovered.

You could say that Knowledge, this deeper Intelligence, is the awareness you had before you came into the world and with it the memory of those who sent you into the world, and the understanding that was given to you to bring you into the world. So different this is, entirely, from your thinking and your beliefs and your philosophies and your ideals. It is an entirely different reality We are talking about here.

Yes, you will try to understand. Yes, you will try to conceptualize. Yes, you will try to fit it in with your current beliefs and attitudes. But, you know, it will not fit, for it is its own reality. You cannot change God into something you want. You cannot change what God has placed within you into something you want or prefer or think you must have.

Now the great truth itself reveals other things that are essential for your understanding. It reveals that you have come into the world at a certain time for a certain purpose. And there are things you must understand about this time that you have come into—things that have not yet been fully realized by even your most visionary and intelligent people in your cultures.

For at this time, humanity is facing the two greatest challenges it will ever face. It will face the challenges of the Great Waves of change—converging Great Waves of change that are all now bearing down on the human family: the disruption of your natural environment; the changing of your weather and climate; the overuse of resources, which are now diminishing in the world; the risk to humanity as food production and social disorder begin to change—the first, declining; the second, increasing. The disruption to your economies, to your beliefs, to your assumptions, to your way of life, will be so substantial and will be global in nature, certainly affecting certain people more than others, but everyone will be impacted.

These Great Waves of change have been set in motion. Some of them now cannot be altered, and you will have to adapt to a very different set of circumstances. Of course, many people will not adapt. They will fight. They will struggle. And thus individuals, groups and nations will face the great temptation of going to war over the remaining resources.

The second great challenge for humanity is its encounter with life from beyond the world, as it stands at the threshold of space. For the world now has become attractive to other races. Humanity has established an infrastructure that other races can use for themselves. And humanity is destroying the natural environment, an environment that is valued by others who seek to use these resources for themselves. For you are the native peoples of this world. This is your planet of origin, but you risk losing it to foreign powers, to competition from beyond.

These two great forces—the Great Waves of change and your encounter with the Greater Community of intelligent life, which includes the Intervention that is occurring in the world at this time by those races who would seek to use humanity for their own benefit—these two great phenomena are related to each other. And this is what awaits you in the future. This is what is beginning to reveal itself to you even now.

People are only beginning to become aware of the Great Waves of change, and many people are still in denial of this or remain ignorant of it altogether. Your encounter with the Greater Community and the reality of Intervention in your world is only known to a very few people in the world.

God would not leave humanity without a preparation for these two great events, events which have the power, either of them, to end human civilization, to alter the fate and destiny and lives of every person in the world.

Therefore, the great truth tells you then that you have come into the world to live in a world that will be undergoing these two great challenges. Whether your specific purpose is to deal with them directly or not, they will create the environment in which you live. They will alter the circumstances of your life. And they will call upon Knowledge within you to emerge.

They—in all of their gravity, in the great threat they pose to human sovereignty and freedom in this world—will in themselves also be a calling to you, a calling to awaken from your dream of self-obsession and self-fulfillment, to awaken from those things that circumscribe you now to respond to a greater reality in your world.

You do not yet realize that these two great challenges, the greatest that have ever faced humanity so far, are the very things that can call out of you the greater purpose that has brought you here, and create a dramatic shift within yourself from a person who is governed by social conditioning to one who is guided by the light of Knowledge.

The great truth of your time is that you will be facing the Great Waves of change and the realities of the Greater Community—the Greater Community which represents intelligent life in the universe and what you as an emerging race must face and learn to understand. For this is a reality that has never been brought to the world in this way before.

You seem pre-eminent in your own world, even though you have been careless stewards of the world itself, but you are a weak and divided race in the Greater Community, and that makes you tremendously vulnerable. You are destroying your ability to be self-sufficient in the future, which also makes you incredibly vulnerable in the universe. You are full of superstition and self-importance and therefore do not realize the real meaning of a foreign presence in your world. You think it is here to gratify you, to save you, or to acknowledge you, and you fail to see it merely represents competition, which in itself is a reality of nature, of the physical reality.

Only God can prepare you for these two great phenomena. You yourself will not know what to do. You may have engaging ideas or promising things that occupy you, but you will not know how to prepare. You do not know what you are preparing for. And should you recognize the real situation, you could be overcome and lose heart, and capitulate and fall into despair.

For without Knowledge to guide you and to lead you through the unpredictable and uncertain future you face, you will either run away and try to hide, or you will fight and become a destructive force in the world, or you will simply fall down and capitulate in despair.

That is why there is a New Message from God in the world, you see, for these great times, this great threshold that humanity is facing. The consequence of its destruction of the world and misuse of the world, and the consequence of its evolution, which eventually would bring it into the Greater Community itself—only God can prepare you for these things. And that is why there is a New Message from God in the world.

Everything that the Creator of all life has given to humanity prior to this, which is of the utmost value and which has only been partially realized and brought to bear, this in itself would not be sufficient to prepare you for the Great Waves of change or for the realities of the Greater Community itself.

Perhaps these two great phenomena do not seem to be relevant to your current thoughts and plans and ideas, but that is because your thoughts and plans and ideas are not grounded in reality. To live in this world, you must prepare to live in the moment and prepare for the future all at once. These are required of you to survive and to prosper under these circumstances—in a world of conflict, in a world of change, in a world of consequence.

Perhaps your greater purpose will only be relevant to serving the needs of one or two people or things that are specific in your environment, but they will all be conditioned by these two great phenomena.

Therefore, the great truth reveals that to understand yourself, you must understand the great events of your time. To understand yourself, you must have this greater perspective, or you will not recognize the context in which Knowledge within you can emerge and prove and demonstrate its relevance and importance to you.

God knows you are not ready. God knows you are preoccupied. You are obsessed with other things. You are reacting to small problems and not responding to great problems. God knows you are not free to follow where Knowledge will lead you and what it will ask of you. God knows what is coming.

You cannot avoid it. To run away and hide only makes you more vulnerable. To pretend it does not exist only renders your life more vulnerable and incapable of responding. To argue and fight against this Revelation is only to show your weakness and your own irresolution. To hold on to what you want is to remain small and weak and incapacitated. Perhaps that worked in the past to some degree, but now it will not be sufficient.

The Great Waves of change are coming. They are already washing up upon your shore. They are already destroying your crops. They are already affecting people around the world. They are already diminishing your security.

And there is a Greater Darkness in the world. There is a foreign presence here that is dangerous for humanity, a presence that presents itself as benign, but which has grave intentions for humanity.

Knowledge within you knows these things. It will respond to these things. And it will respond to everything in your life that can bring you closer to the greater purpose that has brought you here. For the need of your soul, which is far deeper and more substantial than any of your psychological or emotional needs, is to fulfill your purpose in coming. Once you have sufficient food and water and shelter and security, this becomes the focus of your life.

There are many people today who cannot even have this focus, for they do not have the essentials to provide food and water, shelter and security. But for those who do, this is their calling. Service is their purpose for coming.

This is a greater truth about your life. No matter what position you might take regarding it, it remains the great truth about your life. No matter what your attitude regarding the world—your hatred of the world, your repudiation of the world, your anger towards the world—these two great events are taking place and they will determine the future.

How humanity responds, the degree to which humanity can unite in response, the degree to which humanity can end its ceaseless conflicts and prepare to stabilize the world and to prepare for its future in the Greater Community as a free and self-determined race—this represents the one great chance for humanity to unite on its own behalf, to unite out of necessity, to unite because it has no real alternative.

You see, if nations and groups will not unite based on the recognition of the greater truth, then they will be forced to unite under grave circumstances. And if they fail in this, they will simply decline and be overtaken.

Perhaps you feel in this moment an anxiety about the future. Perhaps at this moment you look at the world and you feel great concern. Perhaps at this moment there is uncertainty in your life about what will happen and what you must do.

If this is true in your experience, this is very important, you see. Because these are the signs, within yourself and from the world, that are telling you to beware, to take notice, to focus your attention, to break free of other obsessions and to concentrate on your life and on your relationships and on your ability to prepare for a future that will be unlike the past.

Should you be able to respond adequately here, you will realize that you do not have the answer, that you may only have partial solutions to partial things, but you do not have the answer, that the answer must come from a greater power in your life, a greater power that God has given you, a greater power that resides within you even now.

If you can hear these words, they will begin to give you a clearer view about your life—a deeper understanding of where you are; the change you must bring about; how you must refocus yourself; how you must regard your engagements with the world, your relationships, the security of your family, your culture and the great problems that are now emerging for humanity.

All of these great problems are the reality of nature—the destruction of your life-sustaining system here on Earth and dealing with competition from beyond the world. These are all entirely natural, you see. These are all part of nature. These are all part of life. If you understand nature, you will see that competition is part of nature. And you will see that if you abuse or overuse your environment, it will not be able to sustain you adequately.

There are many solutions that will have to be brought to bear, some of them technological and some of them not. But there must be a great change of heart; a great change of focus; a great rallying of the human spirit; a great uniting of peoples facing common threats, common dangers and a common fate.

This is why there is a New Message from God in the world because there must be a warning, a blessing and a preparation. God will not ignore humanity as it falls prey to its own misbehavior and to the interventions of others. But God can only speak to what God has created within you, and only what God has created in you can fully respond to what God wills for humanity.

It is God's Will for humanity that you restabilize the world, that you find a balance with the world and your use of the world. And it is God's Will that you emerge into a Greater Community of intelligent life as a free and self-determined race.

But you see, what God wills and what people want are not the same. That is why you are living in Separation because you want things for yourself that God did not intend. That is why you are in conflict, and this is the source of all your conflict. This is why the needs of the soul go unmet. This is why you see the world you see. The Will of God must now compete with other intentions, and that creates the reality of life, at the level of physical reality.

Do not think that the outcome simply represents the Will of God, for the outcome will be determined by whether the Will of God can be experienced, expressed and brought to bear, or not. If humanity fails, it fails on its own. If humanity succeeds, it will succeed on its own strengths and on the power that God has placed within each person, the great gift that God has given to a struggling humanity.

You may say, "Well, what about religion? Is the great truth part of what religion teaches?" What religion teaches is in large part what humanity has implemented. Though each religion was born with a pure message and a pure intent, they have all fallen prey to human manipulation; to the manipulation of the state; to the appropriation by selfish, misguided individuals. What is pure remains pure within them all, but what is pure can be difficult to find now. That is why there must be a New Message. And it must be understood and presented in its pure form.

For humanity does not have time now to go through centuries of rejection and adaptation to a New Revelation. You do not have the time. The future of humanity will be determined within the next few decades. You do not have the time.

In your heart, you know this to be true, and that is part of your anxiety, that time now is of the essence—the time you have to realize your greater purpose and calling in the world; to take the Steps to Knowledge; to learn how to discern Knowledge from all the other forces in your mind, all the influences in your life; to let Knowledge guide you; to let Knowledge express itself through you; to let your life be reshaped in the light of Knowledge, which God has given you.

This is not only for your redemption. This represents the real promise and the real strength of humanity. This represents your gift, the gift

of your life and contribution as humanity stands at this great
threshold.

To begin to understand that there is a greater truth, you must see that
this truth exists beyond your ideas and concepts, beyond your fears
and preferences. How it will be recognized, how it will be expressed,
when it will be recognized, when it will be expressed, are all
dependent upon you and others and your circumstances. But the
truth itself remains pure and unassailable.

As you go towards it, your life will begin to feel purposeful and
uniform, meaningful and directed. As you go away from it, you will
feel your life is confused and aggravated, meaningless and full of
difficulty.

For God is the Great Attraction, and what God has placed within you
is what enables you to respond to the Great Attraction of God. It is
like a homing device that leads you in a certain direction; that
stimulates certain activities and expressions; that leads you to give
your life here, not there, to go with these people, not those people; to
respond to this problem and not that problem.

For you are not merely returning to God. You are here to contribute
to the world. This is what redeems you. This is what restores to you
what God has given you and what you truly are.

Why would you escape the world when so much work has been done
to bring you here—to prepare you, to guide you, even when you do
not listen—if you are not here to provide a real service to humanity
and to all life in this world?

There is a greater truth about your life. There is a greater truth about the world. There is a greater truth about your relationship with the world. There is a greater truth about human destiny. There is a greater truth about success and failure. There is a greater truth about the universe.

There is a New Message from God in the world to remind humanity of this greater truth and to give it total relevance to this time and to the times to come.

Be of good cheer, then, for there is a New Revelation in the world. There is a reaffirmation of the reality of humanity's spirit and purpose and destiny. Be affirmed, then, that your concern for the future is appropriate and that your growing need to find your place and your purpose is authentic and must be honored.

Be encouraged that there are great Spiritual Powers in service to the world, and ultimately that God has placed within you an incorruptible Intelligence that you are only now beginning to discover.

CHAPTER 14

You Are Here for a Greater Purpose

As revealed to
Marshall Vian Summers
on August 18, 2008
in Boulder, Colorado

You were sent into the world to make a unique contribution to a world in need. You have come at a time of great change and difficulty for the human family, a time when humanity will have to face Great Waves of change that are coming to the world, all converging at this time.

You have come at a time when humanity is encountering races from beyond the world who are here to take advantage of a weak and divided humanity. You are here to face and to deal with a set of circumstances that your ancestors never had to consider before.

You have come with a greater Knowledge and a greater power, which God has placed within you to be discovered at this time, to emerge at this time—at this great time of uncertainty and upheaval.

While you have a personal mind that has been conditioned by the world, that is full of hopes and fears, judgments and considerations, you have a deeper Intelligence within you that God has placed there. This Intelligence is called Knowledge.

It does not think like your personal mind. It does not judge. It does not deliberate. It does not compare and contrast. It does not use reason and logic, for it is far more powerful than this. People experience it in flashes of intuition, but it itself is greater than intuition.

God knew that you would need the power of Knowledge to be in the world, at this time especially. And everyone in the world has this Knowledge within them, waiting to be discovered. But it is a discovery that only very few have made. And it is essential in these difficult times that many people make this discovery, that you make this discovery.

You are carrying a great strength, unknowingly. Regardless of what you are preoccupied with, or the problems or concerns that you are dealing with at this moment, you were sent into the world to make a unique contribution. You do not yet know what that is, but you have clues. For over the course of your life, there have been indicators and signs and perhaps a growing sense that you are here for something important, but you have not seen what it is yet.

The realization of what this is will come as you take the steps toward Knowledge, as you reconnect with this deeper Intelligence within you that represents the core of your spirituality and your permanent and true nature that God has created.

It is there whether you are religious or not, whether you adhere to a faith tradition or not—no matter what country you are from, no matter what culture or family or village you are from, no matter what your economic status, you are carrying the power of Knowledge within yourself, waiting to be discovered.

This Knowledge is needed in the world now, for humanity will need a greater strength and a greater commitment to navigate the difficult times ahead. Humanity will need a deeper inspiration to overcome the grave anxiety and fear and hostility that will emerge in these unsettled times.

God has given you this strength to see and to know the truth beyond all appearances. But to do this, you must see beyond your judgments and your condemnation. You must give up your avoidance and denial and face a changing world with as much courage and objectivity as you can muster.

Your life is more important than you realize. And the time in which you live is more critical than you might be aware of. Do not shrink from this, or you shrink from your true nature and your true purpose for being here.

It is no accident that you have come at this time—a time of increasing turbulence and uncertainty; a time when humanity will have to face great difficulties in your environment, in politics and religion; great difficulty in securing the fundamental resources that are needed for people to live a stable and secure life.

Beyond your political views and your attitudes is the ability for you to see clearly. But you must clear your vision. You must set aside your ideas and assumptions to have this clarity and to see with this strength.

Knowledge within you will reveal what you must see, know and do. It will restrain you from making mistakes, and from giving your life away to people or things or places that have no real purpose or meaning for your life. And it will encourage you to find those individuals who can recognize your deeper nature and who will be a part of your greater purpose in the world.

Your task now is to discover the power and the presence of Knowledge within your life and to begin to face the world with clarity and sobriety, strength and courage. You know not what you are here to do specifically, but you do know that you are here to do something important. And that is enough to take you to the next step, which will give greater clarity and freedom to your life.

This is a mysterious journey. You cannot figure it out. The path is given to you step by step as you proceed, as you show greater strength and courage and self-trust.

You may doubt yourself, but once you experience Knowledge within yourself, you will see that it is worthy of your trust and devotion. It is beyond your personality. It is a power that you share with all others who have come here at this time. And Knowledge is here to contribute to a world in need and to fulfill you at the deepest level.

This is the power and the presence that you carry within you. And the Message has been sent from God into the world to reveal this power and this presence, and to provide the Steps to Knowledge so that you may find and discover your true strength and purpose and direction with as little loss of time as possible.

This is God's great blessing and endowment. It is awaiting you within yourself and beyond yourself. You will resonate with it once you see it and know it and experience it because it represents the deepest truth about your life.

IMPORTANT TERMS

*T*he New Message from God reveals that our world stands at the greatest threshold in the history and evolution of humanity. At this threshold, God has spoken again, revealing the great change that is coming to the world and our destiny within the Greater Community of life beyond our world, for which we are unaware and unprepared.

Here the Revelation redefines certain familiar terms, but within a greater context and introduces other terms that are new to the human family. It is important to understand these terms when reading the texts of the New Message and hearing the Voice of Revelation.

GOD is revealed in the New Message as the Source and Creator of all life and of countless races in the universe. Here the greater reality of God is unveiled in the expanded context of life in this world and all life in the universe. This greater context redefines the meaning of our understanding of God and of God's Power and Presence in our lives. The New Message states that to understand what God is doing in our world, we must understand what God is doing in the entire universe. This is now being revealed for the first time through a New Message from God. In the New Message, God is not a divine entity, personage or a singular awareness, but instead a pervasive force and presence that permeates all life and is moving all life in the universe towards a state of unity. God speaks to the deepest part of each person through the power of Knowledge that lives within them.

THE SEPARATION is the ongoing state and condition of being separate from God. The Separation began when part of Creation willed to have the freedom to be apart from God, to live in a state of

Separation. As a result, God created our evolving world and the expanding universe as a place for the separated to live in countless forms and places. Before the Separation, all life was in a timeless state of pure union. It is to this original state of union with God that all those living in Separation are ultimately called to return—through relationship, service and the discovery of Knowledge. It is God's mission in our world and throughout the universe to reclaim the separated through Knowledge, which is the part of each individual still connected to God.

KNOWLEDGE is the deeper spiritual Intelligence within each person, waiting to be discovered. Knowledge represents the eternal part of us that has never left God. The New Message speaks of Knowledge as the great hope for humanity, an inner power at the heart of each person that God's New Message is here to reveal and to call forth. This deeper spiritual Intelligence exists beyond our thinking mind and the boundaries of our intellect. It alone has the power to guide each of us to our higher purpose and destined relationships in life. The New Message teaches extensively about the reality and experience of Knowledge.

THE ANGELIC ASSEMBLY is the presence of God's Angels who have been assigned to watch over our world and the evolution of humanity. This Assembly is part of the hierarchy established by God to support the redemption and return of all those living in Separation in the physical reality. Every world where sentient life exists is watched over by an Angelic Assembly. The Assembly overseeing our world is now translating the Will of God for our time into human language and understanding, which is now being revealed through the New Message from God. The term Angelic Assembly is synonymous with the terms Angelic Presence and Angelic Host in the text of the New Message.

THE NEW MESSAGE FROM GOD is a communication from
God to people of all nations and religions. It represents the next stage
of God's progressive Revelation for the human family and comes in
response to the great challenges and needs of humanity today. The
New Message is over 9000 pages in length and is the largest
Revelation ever given to the world, given now to a literate world of
global communication and growing global awareness. The New
Message is not an offshoot or reformation of any past tradition and is
not given for one tribe, nation or group alone. It is God's New
Message for the whole world, which is now facing Great Waves of
environmental, social and political change and the new threshold of
emerging into a Greater Community of intelligent life in the
universe.

THE VOICE OF REVELATION is the united voice of the Angelic
Assembly delivering God's Message through a Messenger sent into
the world for this task. Here the Assembly speaks as one Voice, the
many speaking as one. For the first time in history, you are able to
hear the actual Voice of Revelation speaking through God's
Messenger. It is this Voice that has spoken to all God's Messengers in
the past. The Word and the Sound of the Voice of Revelation are in
the world and are available for you to hear in their original audio
form.

THE MESSENGER is the one chosen, prepared and sent into the
world by the Angelic Assembly to receive the New Message from
God. The Messenger for this time is Marshall Vian Summers.
Marshall is a humble man with no position in the world who has
undergone a long and difficult preparation to receive God's New
Revelation and bring it to the world. He is charged with the great
burden, blessing and responsibility of presenting this Revelation to a
divided and conflicted world. He is the first of God's Messengers to

reveal the reality of a Greater Community of intelligent life in the universe. The Messenger has been engaged in this process of Revelation since the year 1982.

THE PRESENCE refers to different but interconnected realities: the presence of Knowledge within the individual, the Presence of the Angelic Assembly that oversees the world or ultimately the Presence of God in the universe. The presence of these three realities offers a life-changing experience of grace and relationship. All three are connected to the larger process of growth and redemption for us, for the world and for the universe at large. Together they represent the mystery and purpose of our lives, which the New Message reveals to us in the clearest possible terms. The New Revelation offers a modern pathway for experiencing the power of the Presence in your life.

STEPS TO KNOWLEDGE is an ancient book of spiritual practice now being given by God to the world for the first time. Steps provides the lessons and practices necessary for learning and living the New Message from God. In beginning the Steps, you embark on a journey of discovering Knowledge, the mysterious source of your inner power and authority, and with it the essential relationships you are destined to find. Its 365 daily "steps," or practices, lead you to a personal revelation about your life and destiny. In taking this greater journey, you can discover the power of Knowledge and your experience of profound inner knowing, which lead you to your higher purpose and calling in life.

THE GREATER COMMUNITY is the larger universe of intelligent life in which our world has always existed. This Greater Community encompasses all worlds in the universe where sentient life exists, in all states of evolution and development. The New Message reveals that humanity is in an early and adolescent phase of its development and that the time has now come for humanity's emergence into the Greater Community. It is here, standing at the threshold of space, that humanity discovers that it is not alone in the universe, or even within its own world.

THE GREATER COMMUNITY WAY OF KNOWLEDGE is a timeless tradition representing God's work in the universe to reclaim the separated in all worlds through the power of Knowledge that is inherent in all intelligent life. To understand what God is doing in our world, we must begin to understand what God is doing in the entire universe. For the first time in history, The Greater Community Way of Knowledge is being presented to the world through a New Message from God. The New Message opens the portal to this timeless work of God underway throughout the universe in which we live. We stand at the threshold of emerging into this Greater Community and must now have access to The Greater Community Way of Knowledge in order to understand our destiny as a race and successfully navigate the challenges of interacting with life in the universe.

THE INTERVENTION is a dangerous form of contact underway by certain races from the Greater Community who are here to take advantage of a weak and divided humanity. This is occurring at a time when the human family is entering a period of increasing breakdown and disorder, in the face of the Great Waves of change. The Intervention presents itself as a benign and redeeming force while in reality its ultimate goal is to undermine human freedom and self-determination and take control of the world and its resources. The New Message reveals that the Intervention seeks to secretly establish its influence here in the minds and hearts of people at a time of growing confusion, conflict and vulnerability. God is calling us, as the native peoples of this world, to oppose this Intervention, to alert and educate others and to put forth our own rules of engagement as an emerging race. Our response to the Intervention and the Greater Community at large is the one thing that can unite a fractured and divided human family at a time of the greatest need and consequence for our race.

THE GREAT WAVES OF CHANGE are a set of powerful environmental, economic and social forces now converging in the world. The Great Waves are the result of humanity's misuse and overuse of the world, its resources and its environment. The Great Waves have the power to drastically alter the face of the world—producing economic instability, runaway climate change, violent weather and the loss of arable land and freshwater, threatening to produce a world condition of great difficulty and human suffering. The Great Waves are not an end times or apocalyptic event, but instead a challenging period of transition to a new world reality. The New Message reveals what is coming for the world and provides a preparation to enable us to navigate a radically changing world. God is calling for human unity and cooperation born now out of sheer necessity for the preservation and protection of human civilization. Together with the Intervention, the Great Waves represents one of the two great threats facing humanity and a major reason why God has spoken again.

HIGHER PURPOSE refers to the specific contribution each person was sent into the world to make and the unique relationships that will enable the fulfillment of this purpose. Knowledge within the individual holds their higher purpose and destiny for them, which cannot be ascertained by the intellect alone. These must be discovered, followed and expressed in service to others to be fully realized. The world needs the demonstration of this higher purpose from many more people as never before.

196

SPIRITUAL FAMILY refers to the small working groups formed after the Separation to enable all individuals to work towards greater states of union and relationship, undertaking this over a long span of time, culminating in their final return to God. Your Spiritual Family represents the relationships you have reclaimed through Knowledge during your long journey through Separation. Some members of your Spiritual Family are in the world and some are beyond the world. The Spiritual Families are a part of the mysterious Plan of God to free and reunite all those living in Separation.

ANCIENT HOME refers to the reality of life and the state of awareness and relationship you had before entering the world, and to which you will return after your life in the world. Your Ancient Home is a timeless state of connection and relationship with your Spiritual Family, The Assembly and God.

THE STORY OF THE MESSENGER

Marshall Vian Summers is the Messenger for the New Message from God. For over three decades he has been the recipient of a Divine Revelation given to prepare humanity for the great environmental, social and economic changes that are coming to the world and for humanity's contact with intelligent life in the universe.

In 1982, at the age of 33, Marshall Vian Summers was called into the deserts of the American Southwest where he had a direct encounter with the Angelic Presence, who had been guiding and preparing him for his future role and calling. This encounter forever altered the course of his life and initiated him into a deeper relationship with the Angelic Assembly, requiring that he surrender his life to God. This began the long, mysterious process of receiving God's New Message for humanity.

Following this mysterious initiation, he received the first revelations of the New Message from God. Over the decades since, a vast Revelation for humanity has unfolded, at times slowly and at times in great torrents. During these long years, he had to proceed with the support of only a few individuals, not knowing what this growing Revelation would mean and where it would ultimately lead.

The Messenger has walked a long and difficult road to receive and present the largest Revelation ever given to the human family. Still today the Voice of Revelation continues to speak through him as he faces the great challenge of bringing God's New Revelation to a troubled and conflicted world.

Read more about the life and story of the Messenger
Marshall Vian Summers:
www.newmessage.org/story-of-marshall-vian-summers

THE JOURNEY TO A NEW LIFE

Read and hear the original revelation *The Story of the Messenger:*
www.newmessage.org/story-of-the-messenger

Hear and watch the world teachings of the Messenger:
www.newmessage.org/messenger

THE VOICE OF REVELATION

For the first time in history, you can hear the Voice of Revelation, such a Voice as spoke to the prophets and Messengers of the past and is now speaking again through a new Messenger who is in the world today.

The Voice of Revelation is not the voice of one individual, but that of the entire Angelic Assembly speaking together, all as one. Here God communicates beyond words to the Angelic Assembly, who then translate God's Message into human words and language that we can comprehend.

The revelations of this book were originally spoken in this manner by the Voice of Revelation through the Messenger Marshall Vian Summers. This process of Divine Revelation has occurred since 1982. The Revelation continues to this day.

———— ❦ ————

Hear the original audio recordings of the
Voice of Revelation, which is the Source of the text contained
in this book and throughout the New Message:
www.newmessage.org/experience

Learn more about the Voice of Revelation,
what it is and how it speaks through the Messenger:
www.newmessage.org/voiceofrevelation

ABOUT THE SOCIETY FOR THE NEW MESSAGE FROM GOD

Founded in 1992 by Marshall Vian Summers, The Society for the New Message from God is an independent religious 501(c)(3) non-profit organization that is primarily supported by readers and students of the New Message, receiving no sponsorship or revenue from any government or religious organization.

The Society's mission is to bring the New Message from God to people everywhere so that humanity can find its common ground, preserve the Earth, protect human freedom and advance human civilization as we stand at the threshold of great change and a universe full of intelligent life.

Marshall Vian Summers and The Society have been given the immense responsibility of bringing the New Message into the world. The members of The Society are a small group of dedicated individuals who have committed themselves to fulfill this mission. For them, it is both a burden and a great blessing to give themselves wholeheartedly in this great service to humanity.

THE SOCIETY FOR THE NEW MESSAGE

Contact us:

P.O. Box 1724 Boulder, CO 80306-1724
(303) 938-8401 (800) 938-3891
011 303 938 84 01 (International)
(303) 938-1214 (fax)
society@newmessage.org
www.newmessage.org
www.marshallsummers.com
www.alliesofhumanity.org
www.newknowledgelibrary.org

Connect with us:

www.youtube.com/thenewmessagefromgod
www.facebook.com/newmessagefromgod
www.facebook.com/marshallsummers
www.twitter.com/godsnewmessage

Donate to support The Society and join a community of givers who are helping bring the New Message to the world:
www.newmessage.org/donate

ABOUT THE WORLDWIDE COMMUNITY OF THE NEW MESSAGE FROM GOD

The New Message from God is being studied and practiced by people around the world. Representing more than 90 countries and studying the New Message in over 30 languages, a worldwide community of students has formed to both receive the New Message and support the Messenger in bringing God's New Message to the world.

The New Message has the power to awaken the sleeping brilliance in people everywhere and bring new inspiration and wisdom into the lives of people from all nations and faith traditions.

Learn more about the worldwide community of people who are learning and living the New Message and taking the Steps to Knowledge in their lives.

———

Read and hear the original Revelation *The Worldwide Community of God's New Message:*
www.newmessage.org/theworldwidecommunity

Join the free worldwide community site where you can meet other students and engage with the Messenger:
www.community.newmessage.org

Learn more about the educational opportunities available in the Worldwide Community:

Community Site - www.community.newmessage.org
New Message Free School - www.community.newmessage.org/school
Live Internet Broadcasts and International Events -
www.newmessage.org/events

Encampment - www.newmessage.org/encampment
Online Library of Text and Audio -
www.newmessage.org/experience

BOOKS OF THE NEW MESSAGE FROM GOD

God Has Spoken Again

The One God

The New Messenger

The Greater Community

Steps to Knowledge

Greater Community Spirituality

The Great Waves of Change

Life in the Universe

Wisdom from the Greater Community I & II

Secrets of Heaven

Relationships & Higher Purpose

Living The Way of Knowledge

www.ingramcontent.com/pod-product-compliance
Lightning Source LLC
Chambersburg PA
CBHW022017090426

42739CB00006BA/179